W9-BZT-898

The Emotional House

How Redesigning Your Home

Can Change Your Life

KATHRYN L. ROBYN • DAWN RITCHIE

New Harbinger Publications, Inc.

Publisher's Note

This publication is designed to provide accurate and authoritative information in regard to the subject matter covered. It is sold with the understanding that the publisher is not engaged in rendering psychological, financial, legal, or other professional services. If expert assistance or counseling is needed, the services of a competent professional should be sought.

Distributed in Canada by Raincoast Books

Copyright © 2005 by Kathryn L. Robyn and Dawn Ritchie
New Harbinger Publications, Inc.
5674 Shattuck Avenue
Oakland, CA 94609

Cover design by Amy Shoup
Cover image by Julie Toy/The Image Bank/Getty Images
Back cover and interior images by Photodisc/Getty Images
Acquired by Melissa Kirk

ISBN 1-57224-408-9 Paperback

Printed in the United States of America

New Harbinger Publications' website address: www.newharbinger.com

07 06 05

10 9 8 7 6 5 4 3 2 1

First printing

DEDICATED TO RIKI KATSOF

INTREPID REALTOR WHO IS ALWAYS ON THE HUNT FOR
AN EMOTIONAL HOUSE FOR HER CLIENTS

Contents

PART I
YOUR BLUEPRINT

⊰{ 4 }⊱

Life Logistics
Your Factoids
Your Labels
Your Emotional Roller Coasters
Your Coming Attractions
Residence Logistics
What's Lacking in Your House
Existing Problems
Safety and Security Elements
Space and Power Considerations
Planned Alterations

⊰{ 5 }⊱

Saying Who You Are Is a Defining Act
You Can Change Your Life by Changing Just One Room
Defining Yourself
Your New Labels
The Obstacles That Stand in Your Way
Goal Boards—The Great Motivators

⊰{ 6 }⊱

Your Five-Year Life Plan
Your Five-Year House Plan

⊰{ 7 }⊱

Discovering Your Personal Style
The Four Senses
The Fundamentals of Style
Feathering Your Nest
The Color Wheel
Bringing It All Together

PART II
YOUR FOUNDATION

PART III
YOUR HOUSE

Introduction

Studies show it's the emotional brain that controls all your behavior. Even your financial choices are made by your emotions. All these are reflected in your house by the way you design it, decorate it, organize it, and keep it clean. At the same time, every room serves a purpose and tells part of your personal story. In the process of working with clients and writing my first book, *Spiritual Housecleaning: Healing the Space Within by Beautifying the Space Around You* (2001), I discovered that these life stories, in combination with a desire to take control of your life, can empower you to transform your house into a place that helps you take control. So I teamed up with television writer/producer Dawn Ritchie, who brought her production and design experience, to develop a step-by-step program to create a home that gives back and has the power to change your life.

The challenge of making a supportive and inviting home can seem daunting, especially when you don't have the tools or the know-how to do it. But while the majority of us never received professional training in the vagaries of décor, furniture placement, organizing, or design, we've all lived in homes that worked for us and homes that didn't work. And just as we are all more than what we do for a living, more than our hobby, more than the role we play in our families, and more even than who we have been up to now, our homes are more than a roof over our heads in sore need of window treatments. In fact, fixing your home, one room at a time, is like meeting your needs one step at a time, until your very home moves your life into the design you dream for it. This makes your home a new frontier—and that's a good thing. Because everything from personal growth to wholesale change starts right where you live.

—Kathryn Robyn

You may have noticed the abundance of home and garden shows flooding the TV schedule. Whole networks are devoted to the subject—redesigning rooms on meager budgets, organizing, landscaping competitions, and even shows where neighbors risk friendship by making over each others' houses. These series are entertaining to watch, not just for the fabulous design tips, but for the opportunity to witness other people struggling with change. Because after all, a home is the empty space of possibilities in which you write your life.

At the close of many of these shows you get to observe the homeowner's reaction: "Surprise! This is where you live now!" Do they like it, or are they pretending for the camera? Does it work for their lifestyle or does fuchsia carpeting on the walls provoke an asthma attack? Most of the time it's a happy ending, but we—the audience at home—stand in final judgment. What would *you* do differently—change the colors, furniture, or flooring that wouldn't work for your lifestyle? If you're open, this can be an exploration that helps define your own sense of style and being. Would your beloved Siamese cats tear that gorgeous rattan furniture to shreds? Would that inflexible travertine stone flooring wreak havoc with your arthritic hip? Do lavender walls send you into an emotional downward spiral, reminding you of an abusive childhood? Examining your needs before you make physical changes to your living environment is the remedy.

Everyone is unique, and we all see the world through different lenses. Each of us needs a prescription that fits us exactly. This workbook will help get you thinking about what you require in a home, and will give you some tools and rules to follow while walking you through an exploration of your lifestyle and personal taste so you can create a unique prescription for the home that's exactly right for you. Simply put, it's therapy for your home.

—Dawn Ritchie
Los Angeles, 2004

The Emotional House Program

The Emotional House Program is divided into three components: Your Blueprint, Your Foundation, and Your House.

In Part I, **YOUR BLUEPRINT**, you will check your lifestyle baseline by identifying what you love about your house and the problems it presents. Then, by analyzing your emotional needs, you'll uncover what issues you're neglecting that can be addressed by changing something in your home. Next you'll seize the opportunity to define yourself, assess your likes and dislikes, and decide on future goals. Along the way, you'll assemble a basic design kit and samples binder like professional designers do, to help plan your new and improved home.

Your design binder is something you're going to want to keep, because you will use it over and over throughout the years. You'll end up with a permanent collection of furnishing and room measurements, samples of fabric, paint, wallpaper, favorite designs and style types you like, and a great contact list you'll refer to often. If you want to change your curtains to blinds, you need only check your design binder for the inner and outer window frame measurements.

Next, in Part II, **YOUR FOUNDATION**, we will lead you through your house to examine both the practical function and the emotional function of each room, while addressing the current emotional and practical issues in your life. This is where you'll understand why some elements are lacking in your life. Here you'll also learn the House Rules for creating an Emotional House and check your own home for broken rules.

Finally, in Part III, **YOUR HOUSE**, you will tackle your home, room by room, learning the specific rules that apply for each room. You'll set budgets and schedule action plans, with an eye always on the personal goals you defined in the blueprint stage. Then you'll purge or restructure the old and design and decorate the new. Your future shouldn't be limited by an endless list of time-killing chores created by your living environment, so you'll also look at organization and efficiency as part of your restructuring.

Your house is a vital part of your support system. And now you'll have some tools to design it for optimal use. Sound difficult? Don't worry. You're not doing this alone. The exercises and guidelines that follow will escort you toward an understanding of what you want out of your life and the reflections in your home that point the way to get there, as well as the obstacles that keep you from it. They will show you how to tweak or transform your rooms to meet your needs and activate your goals.

Let's start by gathering the practical tools. These will support the emotional process.

Tools You Will Need to Design an Emotional House

- Three-ring binder with pockets
- Set of dividers with tabs to organize each section
- Zippered plastic pencil case
- Plastic inserts for business cards and clippings
- Graph paper
- Journal to make notes in
- Measuring tape
- Scissors
- Glue stick, tape, or stapler
- Pencils, pens, or colored markers
- A willingness to explore yourself
- Theme music (it helps make the willingness easier to bear)

What If You Use a Designer?

If you work with designers, complete the BLUEPRINT section first and convey your results to them. Then look at the **House Rules** to ensure none are broken. If your designer balks, remind them that your aim is to create an Emotional House designed specifically for you, not just a dazzling set of rooms that look great in a magazine. The good designers understand this and will want to enable your vision. The ones who don't should make you turn and run.

❧ 1 ❧

What Is an Emotional House?

If you've ever shopped for a home, you may have heard the phrase "this is an *emotional house*" from some realtors. At first, you might have been stymied by the term: Does the house cry? Is there drama going on behind those screen doors? Actually, what realtors are referring to is a home that has been loved and cared for, down to its details—a major selling point.

An Emotional House is not about the "wow" factor. It's all about the "ahhh" factor: that special feeling you get when you enter a room and suddenly find yourself at ease, welcome to be fully yourself and completely at home. This is a home that functions practically, is organized, is inviting, and is a great place to just settle in and be. An Emotional House carries the heart and soul of the people who live there, because their lifestyle and life principles are important enough to infuse their home with them. The benefit is simple physics: every action has an equal and reciprocal reaction—the house gives back.

"Show houses," which are spaces dressed to impress, do neither. They make both visitor and resident feel like window dressing in a fake environment. The Emotional House, on the other hand, has a kitchen that encourages nurturance and instigates culinary experiment; a bedroom that arouses intimacy and exudes safety and security for the vulnerability of sleep; a bathroom clean enough for the sacred acts of rejuvenation and renewal; a living room that attracts fellowship; a home office that motivates effort; special areas that inspire creativity; and a garden that fills your senses. After all, a house is truly only a home when it reflects and supports the occupants, from entry to attic.

The Four Cornerstones of the Emotional House Program:

Harmony • Balance • Support • Stress-Free Environment

Just as a happy life is the result of many, often-intangible factors, various things come together to make an Emotional House. We have identified four cornerstones, without which anything you try to build will crumble. These are **harmony**, **balance**, **support**, and a **stress-free environment**. This *emotional* atmosphere is at the core of every Emotional House.

Each design or organizing solution you make in your home must meet the four cornerstone criteria or it is not a solution, but the beginning of a new problem. Throughout the book, as you embark on your changes, make a mental note to go down the list of cornerstones and ask yourself—will this new change bring harmony to my home? Is it a choice that results in balance? Does it support the lifestyle and goals of everyone who lives here? Does it help create a stress-free environment? Let's explain with some examples.

HARMONY   BALANCE

THE FOUR CORNERSTONES

SUPPORT   STRESS-FREE ENVIRONMENT

A Practical Example

You would love to have a place to read and watch TV in your home like you used to, but your teenaged son and his pals have taken control of the living room to rehearse their band.

THE PROBLEM—Lack of space for the new task brought into the house.

THE EMOTIONAL FALLOUT—Constant screaming matches. The noise is deafening, and you've lost your fellowship room. But he has a big gig coming up; don't you care about him and his future?

YOUR DECISION—Give in for now to restore harmony to the household. After all, he'll be off to music college next year. And this is his first live performance.

CHECK YOUR CORNERS

Was this is a good decision? Let's see how it affected your cornerstones. By giving in and letting him take control of the living room ...

HAS IT RESTORED HARMONY TO THE HOUSE?— Yes. The fighting is over. Your son is a happy teenager again. This is the loving child you remember. And that drum set fits in surprisingly well with the color scheme of the living room. *Harmony* reigns. Come to think of it, rap does have a poetry to it.

HAS IT BROUGHT BALANCE TO THE SITUATION?—No. He got what he wanted, but the *balance* of the whole house is off without a living room to congregate in. His bandmates scowl when anyone enters "their rehearsal space" and trips over a cord. And now, no one else in the family knows where they're allowed to hang out. That's a one-sided result, not a solution that brings balance.

HAS IT PRESENTED A SUPPORTIVE SOLUTION?— Yes and no. It gives *support* to his goals, but *not* to your needs or the rest of the family's.

HAS IT CREATED A STRESS-FREE ENVIRONMENT?— No. All the equipment has caused congestion and you have to walk through the back hall to get to the kitchen. Not having access to your whole house has made it impossible for the family to have a *stress-free environment*. And without your reading downtime, you are growing irritable, which is affecting intimacy with your spouse. Underneath you are resentful and secretly looking forward to the day your son moves. And that doesn't feel good.

CONCLUSION

Surrendering the living room was not a constructive decision. It looked as though *harmony* had been restored (on the surface), but as soon as one of the cornerstones is cracked, your Emotional House starts to crumble and new issues arise—like potential marriage problems in this case. But every dilemma has a solution, even if it sometimes means moving the problem out the door to another parent's house.

This may seem like an extreme example, but there are parents all over America nodding knowingly right now, wondering what they should have done instead.

Finding a Better Solution

Dividing and multifunctioning a room in the house is usually the answer to the problem of lack of space, especially when a new task is brought into the home. But in the case of excessive noise, there's an added complication. A sound barrier will have to be constructed or the task must be moved to a location where it will not disturb others as much—like the garage or basement. There are many options for soundproofing. The best is to create a small room within a room that contains the sound on all sides. It also gives the musicians the added boost of feeling like they're inside a sound studio. Even a couple sheets of Homasote fiberboard or

Sheetrock could do the trick. Construct it in the rec room or basement and you have doubled the insulation—a floor below, and a soundproof room within a room.

Looking at the issues objectively is the key to coming up with solutions. For further details on how to multifunction a room, flip to chapter 16, House Rule #8: Set Boundaries for Room Use, which offers useful tips.

An *Impractical* Example

If your next decision for your home is more along the lines of a décor or furniture choice, the four cornerstones will still apply. A buttery yellow Berber rug may be in harmony with the textures you are using and give much needed balance to the overall color palette of your room, but if it stands in the way of a stress-free environment because you have indoor/outdoor pets, then it isn't a good choice—it's not practical. That should stop you in your tracks: One cornerstone is cracked, and your Emotional House will collapse—probably in a furrow of worry and a set of limiting restrictions on your beloved and innocent pet.

As you approach any decision, whether décor, organization, or task, always run through the four cornerstones to help you assess your choices. Determine which cornerstones this choice will offend and look at the reasons why. When you see the problem clearly and break it down to the "whys" of the problem, the answers come easier—as in the case of the yellow rug: traffic + dirt = stress. Therefore, buy a darker color. In the rap group example, noise + congestion = room imbalance **x** stress **x** lack of support. Therefore, reassign the band's location and create a sound barrier. And voilà, your Emotional House will be whole again, and everyone gets what they need.

It's easy to think, "No way am I putting a sound studio in my house; it's too much work and he's just a kid." But check back at the cornerstones, realizing that these concepts are the pylons that hold up your Emotional House, the actual and symbolic shelter of your (and your family's) life. And with a little extra effort—okay, maybe a lot of extra effort—you can strengthen that pylon rather than weaken it. Any way you look at it, you're worth it, he's worth it, and the strength of this family is worth it. And you'll know where he is. That alone might be worth it. That's true harmony.

PART I

YOUR BLUEPRINT

❧{ 2 }❧

You Are the Architect of Your Emotional House

A blueprint is the map that you use to build your house. It shows where the things you need in your house will go, so the builder doesn't forget them. This section is where you will identify the unique needs of your particular life—including both practical and intangible needs—and begin drawing out the map that you'll later use in creating an Emotional House designed explicitly *for you*. Here is a quick exercise just to warm you up and get things rolling.

Where's the Emotional House Part of Your Home So Far?

Take a look around your home, as it is right now. Answer the questions below quickly, without too much deliberation.

1. What's your favorite room? _____

2. How does your favorite room make you feel? _____

3. What's in the room that makes you feel treasured? _____

As you move through this book, you will begin to learn how to spread that good feeling you have in your favorite room throughout your entire house. The Emotional House Program's goal is to make every room a favorite room to help support the seven primary aspects of your life: the physical, personal, professional, social, financial, recreational, and spiritual.

4.   Of these seven areas of your life, which one is *really* working right now?

_____

5.   If you put this area in a room in your house, where would it live? _____

6.   Is this your favorite room/least favorite/no opinion? _____

Sometimes the favorite room and the working part of our lives are in sync. Sometimes they're at odds with one another. This can reveal dysfunction that you can heal by working on your house.

One client, Georgie, a successful professional woman who was experiencing difficulty with the personal aspect of her life—finding a romantic partner—discovered that her favorite room was her bedroom, where she spent most of her leisure time, reading, visiting with friends, and watching TV. Her bedroom was a casually comfortable room filled with childhood and parental mementos and a smaller bed appropriate for one. Understanding that this was the room designed for intimacy, Georgie realized she needed to move her casual friends out of her bedroom and transform it into a room that could accommodate a significant other.

But that wasn't the only problem in her home. Appropriate relationships mature through deepening communication, and those activities begin in the room of fellowship and camaraderie (the living room)—consequently the one room she avoided like the plague. Since Georgie wanted a lasting relationship, she didn't want to move immediately to intimacy before progressing through the step of getting to know a suitor. Georgie wanted to concentrate on fixing up her bedroom, but her real work was to unearth the reasons why she didn't feel comfortable in the room meant for fellowship: the living room. For Georgie, part of the answer lay in prominently displayed art pieces given to her by an old beau; these held painful memories and kept her out of that room. Removing those things and taking back the room for herself opened the door for renewed fellowship in the room appropriately designed for that purpose.

7.   What is your least favorite room in your home? _____

8.   What's in that room that gives you an icky feeling?_____

If you don't know, don't worry. You'll get a chance to uncover it later in the program when you engage in the D.U.S.T. exercise.

Some of the goals of the Emotional House Program are: to make every room work to its optimum function, to expand your horizons, and to move you into your whole house. You shouldn't have to secret away your life to just one room. Keep in mind that absolute perfection is impossible and this program isn't a rush to the finish line. Creating an Emotional House is like creating a good life. It's a lifelong commitment. Your home will change with you as you grow.

Hotspot Checklist

Answer these questions in one word. Write down the very first thing that comes to mind.

In your home, which area:

Causes you the most stress? _____

Are you embarrassed about? _____

Is most congested? _____

Is most disorganized? _____

Is least functional? _____

Is the most uncomfortable? _____

Is the most unattractive? _____

Is filthy? _____

Has the most junk? _____

Is used for the wrong function? _____

Needs repair? _____

Is furnished but never used? _____

These are your HOTSPOTS. They may have become the root source of emotional turmoil or may be troubled because of unresolved personal issues. Sometimes it's just a lack of basic homemaking experience that has led you to create a home with these problems. Mostly though, you will discover underlying "emotional dirt" in these areas that is begging to be dealt with. Correcting your HOTSPOTS will assist you in eliminating a great many stressors in your life. So it's worth tackling these areas first. Bear in mind, there's no cause for shame. You can bet that every home you've drooled over in those stunning magazine layouts encloses at least one embarrassing HOTSPOT. The simple truth is: Wherever humans live, their issues are living with them. Now is the time to get a notebook or some loose-leaf paper for your HOUSE JOURNAL. You'll use this throughout the book. Make a heading on the first page named HOTSPOTS and jot your HOTSPOTS down here. You'll come back to them later in chapter 4. In the next chapter you'll be creating your *Emotional House Design Binder*, a good place to keep your HOUSE JOURNAL.

HOUSE JOURNAL

Most chapters in this workbook will include a section that encourages you to explore ideas or thoughts that have come up for you during the process. Try exploring your thoughts by just writing whatever comes to mind without stopping, without thinking about it making sense, without rereading, correcting, or editing what you've just written. You do this by letting go. It's the best way to discover thoughts and feelings hidden inside.

Leave a few blank pages in the front of your HOUSE JOURNAL (after your HOTSPOTS list) for other lists you'll create later. After these, enter your thoughts about the following questions:

1. When I think about the way I live in my house, I realize _____

_____

2. When I think about the way I *want* to live my life, I imagine _____

_____

❊{ 3 }❊

Setting Up Your Emotional House Design Binder

Mapping out your blueprint is the perfect time to set up your *Emotional House Design Binder*. It will help you organize your process by having a single place to collect your design elements, ideas, TO DO lists, and the things you want to remember about the way you live while you move through this book. If you didn't get the materials listed in the Introduction, get them now: a three-ringed binder with pockets, a set of dividers to organize each section, and a soft, zippered pencil case that snaps inside the binder for holding loose items like tile or wood samples. The things that will go inside this handy resource binder are:

- Inspirational magazine clippings
- Paint chips & fabric swatches
- Room & furniture measurements
- Floor plans & room mock-ups
- TO DO lists, budgets & schedules
- Design tips & techniques
- Brochures, art & accessory folios
- Bids & contracts from contractors
- Reliable Referrals and Contact List
- Website favorites
- Your Before-and-After-Photos
- House Journal

Organize First!

Take a moment to organize your binder. Start by creating a section for each room in your particular house. As you work on that room you'll keep your notes, measurements, paint color chips, and any other pertinent information there for future reference. That way you'll have a permanent record of the design elements you used in each room. This is especially helpful when you want to freshen your look by touching up your paint, recovering upholstery, repairing window treatments, or refinishing hardwood floors. It's surprising how quickly you can forget whether water- or oil-based polyurethane was used on the floors, or oil or latex paint on a wall.

Your *Emotional House Design Binder* will help you keep all your long-term projects alive, and you can also use it as a history of your process, with your before-and-after-photos. Whenever you find a contractor or service worker you like, this is where you'll keep their contact information. The same goes for websites you like and your emergency numbers. Your *Emotional House Design Binder* should be a one-stop shop for anything to do with the home. You can store your HOUSE JOURNAL here as well, but if you want to keep this private, you can easily pull it out. If you are using a notebook that doesn't have holes that fit into a binder, you can slip it inside the binder pocket. Don't worry about the other sections for now. You'll add them as we go along through the book.

For more tips on making your *Emotional House Design Binder*, visit our website at www.emotionalhouse.com.

❖{ 4 }❖

Logistics Checklist

"The facts, ma'am, just the facts." The fact is, if you live in a 400-square-foot leather boot, with twelve cats, eighteen children, and on a fixed income, it's hard to change those things without great effort. In most cases it would be easier to move than to even try. The same is true about the way you live in your home. We call these the logistics of your blueprint. Let's identify a few basic facts. First, your life logistics, then your residence logistics. This is where we check your baseline living conditions and personal state of affairs—essential information for designing a home that will meet all your needs.

Life Logistics

Your Factoids

1. I currently live:

- ☐ Alone
- ☐ With a partner
- ☐ With roommates
- ☐ With children
- ☐ With animals
- ☐ With elders

2. Financially, I'm:

- ☐ In debt
- ☐ Living paycheck to paycheck
- ☐ Living on a fixed income
- ☐ Comfortable
- ☐ Very secure
- ☐ Have money to burn

3. I do business:

- ☐ Outside the home
- ☐ From the home
- ☐ Combination of both
- ☐ Don't work

4. My health is:

- ☐ Excellent
- ☐ Compromised
- ☐ I have physical challenges
- ☐ I have weight challenges

5. I travel and leave my home unattended:

- ☐ Frequently
- ☐ Infrequently

Your Labels

Everyone has labels they assume—personal, professional, and social. Job titles, family roles, social pigeonholing, personality traits, etc. So let's take a look at yours.

1. List five of the defining labels or titles you currently hold. *For example: parent, wife, sister, Olympian, executive, traveler, student, amateur photographer, salesperson, most valuable player, conservationist, etc.*

    _____

    _____

    _____

    _____

    _____

2. Choose five descriptive words that fit your personality. *For example: funny, driven, angry, relaxed, musical, devoted, creative, talented, lazy, resourceful, playful, athletic, smart, political, etc.*

    _____

    _____

    _____

    _____

    _____

3. Name five action words that describe your daily activities. *For example: run, study, cook, fight, paint, fix, sell, sew, sing, fly, plow, swim, etc.*

    _____

    _____

    _____

    _____

    _____

4. Describe five positive qualities you have. *For example: generous, fair, good listener, talented, warm, reliable, enthusiastic, studious, decisive, loyal, etc.*

    _____

    _____

    _____

    _____

    _____

5. Describe five shadow or negative qualities you have. *For example: don't listen, pushy,
intolerant, selfish, judgmental, uncompassionate,
arrogant, ignorant, bigoted, rigid, stubborn, etc.*

_____

_____

_____

_____

_____

_____

6. Complete this sentence: I'm really good at _____

7. Complete this sentence: What I really love to do is_____

8. Complete this sentence: If I had the job I really wanted, it would be _____

9. Complete this sentence: If I were world-famous, I would be _____

10. Okay, this is the hard part: Tell a secret about yourself, to yourself. The truth is, I _____

_____

11. What words keep popping up repeatedly? _____

12. What themes keep coming up? _____

Look back at all the words you wrote in questions 1 through 9. Repeat them aloud.
Shuffle the words around and play with them. Write them *all* down together here:

_____

_____

_____

_____

_____

_____

Repeat them aloud again. This is the poem of your current life. Inside these words are your dreams, your responsibilities, and your essence. It is one *current* definition of who you are. Does it sound like the person you want to be or the life you want to be living? Keep your Life Poem in your HOUSE JOURNAL. Do this exercise annually and you'll see your life story poetically unfold before you, revealing your progress or where you are stuck.

Your Emotional Roller Coasters

This is the third element of your life logistics, your emotional struggles. Everyone has them. It's time to get clear about what's not working and what's missing in your life. Go down the list. Check all that apply:

1. Do you struggle with:

   ☑ Guilt or resentment   ☐ Eating disorders

   ☐ Weight issues   ☑ A lack of support

   The *kitchen* is your support center where these problems are created as well as healed.

2. Are you afflicted by:

   ☑ Fearfulness   ☐ Allergies

   ☑ Exhaustion   ☐ Insomnia

   ☐ Illness   ☐ Intimacy problems

   The *bedroom*, which should be your sanctuary, is where these issues often land.

3. Are you longing for:

   ☑ Friends   ☑ A feeling of belonging

   ☑ Fun   ☑ Better communication

   The *living room* is where you develop your social graces and where these problems show up.

4. Do you feel:

   ☐ Detached   ☐ Rushed

   ☑ Tense   ☑ Agitated

   The *garden* is the place to find serenity and connectedness to life.

5. Are you suffering with:

- ☐ A lack of motivation
- ☑ Feeling unfulfilled
- ☐ Creative blocks
- ☐ Inability to prioritize
- ☐ Problems getting work
- ☑ Debt or money problems

These issues often arise when you don't have a viable workspace, like a *home office*.

6. Do you need help with:

- ☐ Personal presentation
- ☑ Body image
- ☐ Dignity
- ☑ Spiritual malaise

The *bathroom* is ground zero for these problems and the place to upgrade for an uplift.

7. Are your concerns ones of:

- ☐ Authority
- ☑ Difficulty bonding
- ☐ Sexual temptation
- ☑ Seeking gratification by shopping

The *dining room* is the room where the seeds of these matters are sown and mended.

8. Are you:

- ☑ Angry
- ☑ Overworked
- ☐ Never alone
- ☑ In desperate need of downtime

Then you need a *room of your own* in your home, to unwind and re-center yourself.

9. When you arrive home do you:

- ☐ Instantly feel lonely
- ☐ Find yourself tensing up
- ☑ Immediately start yelling
- ☐ Want to turn around and leave

Your entryway or *foyer* is where these emotions get their start.

10. Are you:

- ☐ Scattered
- ☐ Chronically late
- ☐ A pack rat
- ☐ Unorganized

Your *closets, garage, and storage* areas can be the HOTSPOTS for these troubles.

These are your life logistics. You may have noticed that depression as well as emotional, physical, and sexual abuses are not listed in the emotional roller coasters. That's because they can originate in any room in your house, and accordingly are healed in every room of an Emotional House.

Working with clients on their healing issues or their homes, it became apparent that the problems in their lives were commonly mirrored in their homes. Clients who felt they had no support had unsatisfactory if not unclean kitchens, the heart of a support structure. Others, who had lost the intimacy in their marriage, hadn't set room boundaries and allowed their children free rein of the house, including unrestricted access to their bedrooms and private time. And even when the client was willing, many didn't quite know where or how to start making changes in their lives. Your personal demons and dragons are everywhere in your home, and taming them is an ongoing work in progress.

Make a page called EMOTIONAL ROLLER COASTER ROOMS in your HOUSE JOURNAL. Jot down any emotional roller coasters you ticked off above and write the corresponding room beside them. These rooms will need adjustments.

Your Coming Attractions

It's clearer where you currently stand now, but life almost never remains static. Our circumstances are constantly changing and we have to adapt. Your home should also evolve with the changes in your life and your plans for the future. To smooth the transition to a new situation, you must first make space for it, whether it's preplanning for a newborn or a career change. It lessens the stress of the evolution. However, life sometimes happens faster than home improvement can keep up. So, take a look at the issues about to affect your home.

In the near future my home will have to adjust due to changes in my:

- ❑ Marital or relationship status
- ❑ Number of children at home
- ❑ Elders needing care
- ❑ Career focus or status
- ❑ Where I conduct business

- ❑ Health & fitness needs
- ❑ Financial situation
- ❑ Travel circumstances
- ❑ Companion pets
- ❑ Projects & new hobbies

If you are dealing with a weight issue, for instance, you might need to make room for fitness equipment or new kitchen apparatus. If children are leaving home, you may be reacquiring a room you can convert into a long-anticipated studio or a workspace to begin a small business that will increase your income. Perhaps you have an aging parent who needs your in-home care or you are about to have an operation yourself that requires health apparatus. Or maybe you have a job that is taking you out of town, leaving your home, pets, and plants frequently unattended, and you need to find a responsible house sitter. All these and other issues will require adjustments in your living conditions. Taking your personal inventory is the key to preparation. Make a note of your COMING ATTRACTIONS in the front pages of your HOUSE JOURNAL—you'll use it later in your house plan.

Now onto your residential logistics.

Residence Logistics

How do you want to live? With peace and quiet or with joyful noise? Most of us would probably insist we want both, a balance. If, instead, your life swings between mute isolation and pandemonium, it's possible you have created neither the space for peace, nor the room for noise. So let's take a look at your residence logistics to unearth the physical issues.

What's Lacking in Your House?

1. Put a checkmark beside anything that is lacking in your current home.

☑ Storage space	☐ Play/creative areas	☑ Security system
☐ Meal-prep space	☑ Cupboards	☐ Insulation
☑ Suitable seating	☑ 3-prong power outlets	☐ Air circulation
☐ Adequate lighting		☐ Dishwasher
☐ Adult-only areas	☐ Phone jacks/cable/Internet	☐ Heating alternatives
☐ A good bed		☑ Garden area
☐ Private space	☑ Bill paying area & filing space	☑ Beauty
☐ Enough hot water	☑ Enough bathrooms	☑ Work space
☐ Sound plumbing	☐ Enough bedrooms	☐ Wireless technology
☐ Washer/dryer	☐ Parking spaces	☐ Quietude

Existing Problems

2. Which of the following are existing problems:

- ☐ Crowded quarters
- ☑ Inadequate cooling & heating
- ☐ Household/construction dust
- ☐ Humidity/dryness
- ☐ Pests (rodents/insects/termites)
- ☐ Annoying neighbors
- ☐ Toxicity (carbon monoxide, radon, asbestos)

- ☑ Mold/mildew
- ☐ Noise
- ☐ Too much light in bedroom
- ☐ Lack of privacy
- ☑ Clutter & disorganization
- ☑ Structural damage
- ☑ Water damage/leaks

Safety and Security Elements

3. Which safety and security elements are missing from your home?

- ☑ Deadbolt door locks
- ☑ Window locks
- ☑ Alarm system
- ☑ Security lighting
- ☑ Smoke & carbon monoxide detectors
- ☑ Fire extinguisher & escape ladder

- ☐ Trimmed bushes
- ☑ Well-lit entries & pathways
- ☑ Reliable house sitter
- ☑ Gas & water shutoff valves
- ☑ Internet firewall
- ☐ Baby-safe products

Space and Power Considerations

4. The area of your home with:

The highest traffic is _living/kit_

The least closet space is _kitch?_

The fewest power outlets is _Bed/Bath_

5. The rooms that currently do double duty are _Dining/Liv_

6. The extra rooms you really need in your home are _garden/exercis office_

These are just *some* of the facts that you need to think about while creating the blueprint for a balanced and supportive house. Knowing the logistics and limits of your space and problem areas helps you make decisions about effort, budget, style, convenience, and organization by drawing boundaries around the kinds of changes you can reasonably make in your life and house.

Finding solutions begins by identifying the specific problems, prioritizing them, and creating an action plan with a budget and a schedule. There's not much you can do about annoying neighbors except build strong fences or move away (something you should do if they escalate tensions). But many issues in a home can be agreeably addressed by acquiring services and equipment, by adjusting furniture placement and organization—which includes storage solutions—or with a new coat of paint and the addition of art and accessories for a room.

Create a section called HOUSE PLAN in your *Emotional House Design Binder* and make a note of any of the problems you checked above. Put them in order of their priority. Anything that deals with structural issues comes first (plumbing, termites, mold, etc.). Second is security and safety. (You *especially* need to address this if you have children or noted in the Factoid section that you travel frequently.) Next is space allocation, organization, and equipment, followed by aesthetics and décor. Later, in chapter 21, A Journey Through Your Home, you'll learn how to create an action plan, budget, time limit, and schedule to remedy these problems.

Planned Alterations

7. Which alterations will you want to concentrate on right away?

☑ Cleaning & organization	☐ New equipment
☐ Furniture placement	☐ Beauty & art elements
☐ Design & décor	☐ Power
☐ Room additions	☐ Lighting
☐ Lighting & positioning	☐ Heat & airflow
☑ Comfort elements	☐ Repairs & upgrades
☐ Pest & noise control	☑ Safety & security

As you continue going through the checklists and exercises ahead, you'll be training your eye to see your home in a fresh way—by breaking it down into its parts. This deconstruction process will identify your current assets and essential needs. For example, if you discover the necessity for a home office with a lot of electronic demands to realize a new career path, you won't want to choose a space in your home that has only one power outlet; that is, unless you have the funds to hire an electrician. The same applies to organizing issues. If there is a lack of closet space in your home, you will need to add storage units, containers, and shelving in the proper areas to defeat the junk buildup, or move a function to another room that has ample storage. It is easier to make decisions and changes when you're still in the planning stage than when your life is upended by construction work. Separating the whole into the building blocks of your life and home makes it easier to become the chief architect of your Emotional House.

What issues need a better balance in your life? What changes can you make in your house to support that balance? Take a few minutes to explore ideas and possibilities.

_____

_____

_____

Only you know if you laugh enough, if you cry enough, if you go to sleep at night satisfied that the day was full enough and wake up in the morning ready to face the challenges of a new day. Only you know who's going to take your call when you're in trouble in the middle of the night and who's going to crow with you when you've won bragging rights and not dampen the moment at all. You know if you've done what you intended with the gifts you were born with, or given back what you could have with the gifts that you've enjoyed; if you've reached deeply enough within to feel or far enough outside to care. Only you know if the people who depend on you are wise to do so, or whether those upon whom you depend are worthy.

These questions are the stuff of life. If you've been too easy on yourself or too hard, think how you can balance that out. You can't be perfect, but you should be alive and growing.

❧ 5 ❧

You Are How You Live

How you live defines *who you are*. Not just to yourself, but to others as well. Your home can indisputably affect your position in the world and the quality of your relationships. If your home is in chaos, you are likely often late for work or events. You might feel frustrated—in a constant rush for time, forever feeling pressured by those around you. Others will soon classify you as tardy and unreliable, and your status will quickly diminish. No one wants that. But your home defines you in other ways as well. The design and functionality send you daily messages about your talents, your work, your relationships, and your worthiness.

Be candid and answer these three questions:

1. The message my home gives to visitors is _____

2. The message my home gives to me is _____

3. The message I want to be giving to the world and myself is _____

Your home shouldn't define you in negative or limiting ways; rather it should support you, enliven you, and move you toward greater personal growth and a brighter future. You start creating an Emotional House—one that supports you instead of weakening you—by shaking loose from the old labels that don't fit, defining yourself and your dreams, and making room for that in your home.

Saying Who You Are Is a Defining Act

With each profession or life choice comes a general set of standards. Whether it's becoming a physician or a parent; a spouse or a mechanic; an artist or a salesperson, there is a language you will have to learn, a manner of being you'll have to adopt to achieve credibility, an accepted standard of dress you'll have to adjust to, a set of tools and equipment you will have to acquire, and *a way of living* you'll have to adopt. But saying who you are is the first step.

A colleague, Robert, who wanted to become a writer, had difficulty owning the label. He surrounded himself with a community of budding writers facing the same challenges, wrote whenever he could in a local coffee shop, studied and honed his craft, and shared his work with an open mind to tough criticism. Becoming a professional writer was his goal. Robert was devoted and prolific but still felt like a wannabe.

His fellow writers advised him to start introducing himself as a writer. Robert tried that on for size, but it felt false every time he said it because he had not yet been paid for his service. In his mind, it was what he *wanted* to be, not who he *was*. Despite his misgivings, he forced himself to continue claiming the moniker as his own, admittedly almost choking on the word for a while. But it got easier over time. Eventually the words "I'm a writer" began to roll off his tongue, and he suddenly realized he needed a proper writing desk at home.

You Can Change Your Life by Changing Just One Room

Robert emptied the large walk-in closet in his tiny apartment and converted it into a makeshift office, filling it with writing tools and good lighting. With that, he fully took on the mantle of being a writer. Now he could devote himself to the task every day and write late into the night—which was the time he felt most creative. His need for a private space designed specifically for the life he wanted to lead would help him realize his future. When he finally did begin "taking meetings" and interviewing for writing jobs, he was ready. There was no doubt in his mind who he was or what he was capable of. He dressed like a writer, spoke like a writer, had the tools of a writer, lived the life of a writer, and now that's just who he was.

Saying who you are *is* a defining act. And it is a powerful one. It will lead to positive emotional and physical changes in your living environment. Every day you tell yourself who you are, not just by what you say about yourself and how you dress, but also by how you live. These are the messages you give to yourself and also broadcast to the world. The same is true if it's a relationship you're longing for, someone with whom to share your life. If your home is clearly designed for one, then you aren't making room for the possibility of finding that someone and instead are reinforcing the single message to both yourself and everyone who crosses your threshold. If that's not the message you want to convey, then you need to rethink your design. So, what do you want? Take a leap and define yourself now.

Defining Yourself

Check back to the Life Logistics section at the beginning of the previous chapter. Remember those labels you identified? Take another quick look at them and answer the following questions:

1. If any, which labels don't feel like the real you?

    _____   _____   _____

2. Name the *one* label or title you most wish you held right now instead. *For example: spouse, home-owner, parent, vice president, realtor, honor student, musician, business owner, independently wealthy, etc.*

    _____

3. List three goals you want to reach. *For example: earn a degree, get a pilot's license, own a home, become a parent, get out of debt, sing a solo in the church choir, change jobs.*

    _____   _____   _____

    Does the label you wish you held right now correspond to a goal? If it doesn't, there is a new goal you should set. Take a look around your home. Is there evidence of this person in your existing home setup? There should be.

    You don't have to be a young, aspiring writer like Robert to change your home to fit your dream. Dreams can be realized at any age. If you're a mature adult who has always dreamed of being a blues musician, for instance, you could start acquiring the equipment you need—bass guitar, song sheets, music stand, etc.—and making space in your home for daily practice *today*.

    Crissy did exactly that. She was a fifty-four-year-old middle manager in a large publishing company who took early retirement. She got a guitar, created a music corner in her home with shelving for her song sheets, a crescent of chairs, and music stands, and practiced every day—much to the consternation of some of her less supportive retirement-age friends. Happily, Crissy remained undeterred, joined a group called the Struck Band, and played gigs in small venues in New York City. She continues to experience a very fulfilling new vocation.

Remember, there's no judge here, and wishes count; there are no right or wrong answers, only *your* answers, only *today's* answers. But if you went negative on any of these questions or found the exercise too difficult, go back and try it again. Your home is the one place you shouldn't have to hide. It's a major step in creating an Emotional House.

Let's start the ball rolling. What can you do on the home front to begin to wear that new label or reach that new goal?

4. Name three items you would definitely "have to own" in your home if you'd *already* met your top number one goal. It may be a desk, sewing machine, fitness equipment, tools, etc.

    _____   _____   _____

5. Name one thing in your house that you'd definitely "have to get rid of" if you'd *already* met your top number one goal. It could be clutter, toys in the living room, music equipment in the spare room, a twin bed, a threadbare rug, etc.

    _____

6. Name the room that will have to change to accommodate this new label you *now* own.

    _____

Congratulations! Completing this exercise was a huge move toward changing your life. You've created the beginnings of your map toward an important goal, and you have a brief list of actions you can take in your own home, the one place you deserve command over.

Keep these goals alive in your mind. Create a section named GOALS in your HOUSE JOURNAL. Jot down these goals and make a note of the things you need to acquire, things you need to get rid of, and rooms you believe might have to change to accommodate this new goal. You'll come back to these in the next chapter.

Doing this exercise periodically as you work through this book will help you refine more clearly your essential inner needs and the true character buried beneath old labels or the expectations of others. As you make changes you may still have to own some of the labels that don't feel like the real you out of personal duty, especially if they involve children, elders, or animals you care for, or if you have a health or financial situation you are coping with, but along the way you will be able to aim more directly at the new labels, which also define you.

Own who you are at home, and you will send the ripples of your true spirit outward—into both your professional and social circles. Every giant snowman began with a mere small handful of snow, so take a baby step toward your goal today. Then take another step, and then another tomorrow. That is how you start to gather mass.

The Obstacles That Stand in Your Way

There are always obstacles and there is always a way around them. If you find yourself banging headlong up against a wall you're trying to climb, consider another approach. Move sideways and you might find a way around the wall instead.

Let's look at one possible obstacle. Remember, you have to take a hard look at how you are living, because how you live defines who you are. Flip back to the list of HOTSPOTS that you noted on the first page of your HOUSE JOURNAL (if you didn't do this exercise on page 13 in chapter 2, go back to that section and do it now).

1.   The HOTSPOT in my house that impedes a goal of mine is _____

2.   The resources I already have to change this are _____

3.   The resources I still need are _____

Resources include money, helpers, and even that old furniture and paint you have stored in the garage. Clearing out old junk and holding a yard sale is a great way to acquire additional financial resources when you don't have any.

1.   The *practical* obstacles standing in my way are _____

2.   The *emotional* obstacles blocking me from taking action are _____

Practical obstacles include lack of space or the simple know-how needed to change things. Emotional obstacles are other people who fight you, as well as your own defeating emotions.

In the chapters ahead, you will gain tools like chore charts to help set boundaries with others, methods to multifunction spaces, and processes to dig out the emotional dirt holding you back. House Rule #2: Keep it Clean (chapter 10) will introduce you to the D.U.S.T. principle, a straightforward method to help you unearth the emotional complexities that have manifested limiting conditions in your home. For a more in-depth exploration, you'll want to read Kathryn's previous book, *Spiritual Housecleaning: Healing the Space Within by Beautifying the Space Around You,* (New Harbinger Publications, 2001), which focuses entirely on this subject.

Goal Boards—The Great Motivators

Add to your goals planning by creating a GOAL PICTURE BOARD. This is a very effective tool. Buy a piece of poster board and fill it with photographs and words you clip from magazines that remind you of what you want.

Start today by cutting out pictures from magazines that remind you of the label or title you most wish you had right now, the three goals you've said you want to reach, and the three things you named on page 32 that would be in your home if you'd already met your top number one goal. Visual images are very powerful inspirational motivators.

Hang your goal picture board in a prominent place where you can see it every day (your home office is a great spot). Then start casually browsing and window shopping for these three things for your home. But don't buy quite yet. Later in the book, you will begin taking the first steps toward reaching your goals by making a more detailed action plan to effectively incorporate them into your home and help you realize your full potential.

Remember, it is the rare individual who is to the manor born, but there's no reason you cannot rise to your proper station in life. We are all created with staggering potential. Increasing your personal wealth, enhancing your relationships, and stepping up to your professional and creative power is possible. And it all inevitably starts at home by designing an environment that builds you up, rather than shooting you down.

HOUSE JOURNAL

Are you beginning to see your life in your house? This is hard work you're doing. You might want to use this page to release some of the heebie-jeebies that dissecting your life may have left you with. Take a moment to write about the unproductive or limiting personal issues you now realize you may be nurturing in your home.

_____

_____

_____

_____

❧{ 6 }❧

The Five-Year Plan

Everyone should have a five-year plan. If you don't, make one today and be sure to revise it completely once a year. New Year's Day is a good time, as is your birthday. It's very focusing to take a quick look at all aspects of your life to see where you've set goals and where you've neglected them. It helps in the creation of your blueprint. Knowing what you want and where you're going is essential information for creating an Emotional House that supports that path in its totality. Here's your list of items:

1. PERSONAL: romantic, family, children

2. PROFESSIONAL: work, education, training

3. HOUSING: location, dwelling

4. FINANCIAL: income, savings, investments

5. RECREATIONAL: travel, hobbies, creative expression, entertainment

6. PHYSICAL: Health and fitness, weight, wellness

7. SOCIAL: friends, community

8. SPIRITUAL LIFE: emotional growth, spiritual development, charity

Housing is a basic but very important item in this inventory of human needs, and several other items on the list will impact your choice there. Start your plan at Year 5 by jotting what you want to have or where you want to be within five years. Then work back from there to Year 1 in a progressive fashion. It's the fastest way to set a quick goal list. The plan itself will show you the points along that path that you need to get to each year. If it doesn't direct you to a lifestyle that is attractive to you, then rethink your endpoint.

Life Plan—A Sample

Here's a sample five-year plan for a woman who is a single, fun-loving student right now but wants to move toward a profession, marriage, family, and owning a home in five years. Look at her Year 5 goals first, then see where she went with it.

SAMPLE FIVE-YEAR LIFE PLAN

	YEAR 1	YEAR 2	YEAR 3	YEAR 4	YEAR 5
Personal	Dating	Engaged	Married	Pregnant	Married, 1 child
Professional	College	Graduate School	Graduate School	Environmental lobbyist	Senator's aide
Housing	Dorm	Single Apt.	1-Bed apt.	2-Bed apt.	Own house
Finances	School loan	Scholarship	Scholarship	$50,000 salary	$65,000 salary
Travel & Recreation	Spring break in Florida	Grand Canyon	Hawaii honeymoon	Cottage trip	Holidays in Denver
Health & Fitness	Lose 5 lbs.	Lose 8 lbs.	Quit smoking & maintain weight loss	Smoke free, prenatal care	Fit, swim daily
Social	Frat parties	Become Big Sister	Lead environ. watch group	Volunteer at autism center	Close-knit circle of friends
Spiritual Life	Meditation retreat	Keep a gratitude journal	Attend self-help center	Join church	Member of prayer group

The social, spiritual, health, and recreational goals seem fairly reasonable and doable. But the plan is a jolting reality check in terms of financial, professional, housing, and personal goals. This woman's plan tells her if she wants to ease her way financially with a scholarship, she'll need to finish her undergraduate education near the top of her class. This leads to becoming advantageously employed and saving money toward that house down payment. All this, *and* she wants to start a family within five years. That's why she reconsidered partying every night with the bad boys at the college dorm, as she's doing in Year 1 and opted for a quieter apartment life in Year 2 of her plan. She needed to hit the books hard and get serious about getting a scholarship, as well as begin seeking realistic partners for her future.

Her fun but distracting living environment was defining her future—and that wouldn't be home ownership and a family within five years unless she made a change.

Okay, now it's your turn. Your goals may not be as far-reaching as the example, but defining them is equally important. Take a look at the goals you noted in your HOUSE JOURNAL in the last chapter. These include the labels and titles you wish you owned. You will want to incorporate these into your FIVE-YEAR LIFE PLAN. And there's another area you won't want to leave out. In chapter 4, you defined your current baseline "Factoids." If debt, weight, or health challenges were problems for you on this list, you'll want to set positive goals for a better future in your FIVE-YEAR LIFE PLAN. There are ways to approach these problems in your house.

Okay. Put on a timer and complete Year 5 in three minutes or less. This is where you want to be in five years. Fill each box in with just one or two words. Be creative and be specific. Keep it simple. Keep it short. Keep it fun. Go!

YOUR FIVE-YEAR LIFE PLAN

	YEAR 1	YEAR 2	YEAR 3	YEAR 4	YEAR 5
Personal (romantic, family & children)					
Professional (work, career, education & training)					
Housing (location & dwelling)					
Finances (income, savings & investments)					
Travel & Recreation (vacation, hobbies, creative expression & entertainment)					
Health & Fitness (weight, fitness & wellness)					
Social (friends & community)					
Spiritual Life (emotional & spiritual development, charity, caring for others)					

Okay, now take a look at what you entered for Year 5. Did you cover every base on the chart? If you had difficulty completing a section, that's the area in your life that most needs work. Take another two minutes to explore any sections you had difficulty with. Then, when you're finished with that, put the timer on for another ten minutes and work your way backward from Year 4 to Year 1, filling in the steps along the path. Go!

You might find that took longer. It is interesting to discover that defining the steps along the way takes much more time than setting the original goal. That's why you have to develop an enjoyment of the process of life, not just the final results—the simple truth is, *most* of life is process.

Now take a deeper look at Year 1, the place you are moving toward right now. Does your current living situation—and the COMING ATTRACTIONS you noted in your HOUSE JOURNAL—fall into place for your Year 5 goals, or do you have to make changes to accommodate both your present and your future? No one said changing is easy. Changes are difficult, but they are worth the effort. They freshen your experience and can help you reshape and reframe your life and living situation.

The FIVE-YEAR LIFE PLAN is an insightful tool for quick goal setting and spirited wish making. Be bold and dream big. Jotting it all down in five minutes or less allows you to be surprised at how much you know about yourself already and how interesting you truly are.

Be sure to keep your old plans to see where you've been and where you're headed as you mature. Priorities change with age. The domino effect is remarkable. Check off things you've achieved, or just marvel at the fascinating route your winding path has taken over the years.

If you had difficulty creating a plan, it may be because you are not a results-oriented individual. You may be more process driven. Which means your goals aspire toward an outlook more than a destination. If you are process oriented, adjust your goals to reflect the *experience* you want to have instead of the exact result. For instance, in Year 5 your goal may be to be free of financial worries instead of defining your earnings as a number. Or you may want to reach mastery in work, progressing from journeyman status in Year 1. Perhaps you want personal confidence, pride in yourself or your partner or children, or to live in the country, have job security, trusted friends, etc. This is *your* FIVE-YEAR LIFE PLAN, so you should design it specifically to suit your individual style. When you're finished, tack up a copy where you can see it daily to keep your plan alive in your mind. And keep an extra copy in the GOALS section of your HOUSE JOURNAL.

House Plan

Is your house keeping up with your FIVE-YEAR LIFE PLAN? Now that you've done one for yourself, complete one for your home. Homes require upkeep as well as freshening, and that includes paint. When you have an upkeep and design plan for your home, things get done. Five years can really whiz past, and if you haven't prepared steps by working back from your goals, you'll never get that fence built or that new landscaping done and you'll live with old linoleum and dirty walls for decades.

Take a look back at your priorities list that you put in the HOUSE PLAN section of your *Emotional House Design Binder* to see what needs to go on the list. Be sure to incorporate your COMING ATTRACTIONS and your personal goals. If debt or work is a problem, spend effort on that home office or studio. If weight and fitness are issues, concentrate on creating a fitness area and spaces that fill your spirit instead of your stomach—like your living room, where fellowship should be a nourishing experience. When you're finished, add your five-year house plan to the HOUSE PLAN section of your *Emotional House Design Binder*. Put on the timer for ten minutes. Go!

YOUR FIVE-YEAR HOUSE PLAN

	YEAR 1	YEAR 2	YEAR 3	YEAR 4	YEAR 5
Kitchen appliances, counters, dishes, organization, paint, art, dinette suite, flooring, repairs, etc.					
Living Room furniture, rugs, art, paint, electronics, home theater, repairs, etc.					
Master Bedroom closets, dressers, furnishings, rugs, art, paint, linens, etc.					
Bathroom tiles, porcelain, shower, altar, paint, art, spa items, skylight, etc.					
Home Office computer, bookcases, broadband Internet, printers, fax machine, postal scale, software, files, accounting system, art, paint, etc.					
Garden/Patio plantings, water features, dining area, tree house, pool, chaise longues, umbrella, BBQ, outdoor games, etc.					
Kids' Rooms built-ins, new beds, nursery, desks, computers, linens, paint, art, etc.					
Garage convert, enlarge, add work space, tool bench, storage solutions, repairs, automatic door opener, office, etc.					

❧{ 7 }❧

Possessing Personal Style

Part of creating an Emotional House is imbuing your living environment with your own distinct style and personality. When surrounded with comforting personal items, colors and textures you love, furnishings that work for you—not against you—and art and accessories that inspire, you feel less stressed, more at home, more balanced, more ... *you*. Your home is the canvas of your life, so make sure you make it a work of art. Every corner of your home should be a composition.

Discovering Your Personal Style

You have a personal style, even if you don't know what it is. Exploration is how you discover it. Most people know what kind of movie they prefer—whodunits, romantic comedies, action, art films—because they've sampled them and paid attention to their reactions. Alone in the shadows of a dark theater you were allowed an anonymous cathartic experience, which helped whittle down the choices to reveal your particular taste.

The same approach applies to understanding and developing your design style. Checking in with what you relate to is the secret to discerning your individual taste. Answer these questions.

How do you feel about:

	Love It	Hate It	It's Okay	Don't Know
Patterned wallpaper	☐	☑	☐	☐
Leather couches	☐	☑	☐	☐
Flowery wicker chairs	☐	☑	☐	☐
Sheer café curtains	☐	☐	☑	☐
Ornately carved picture frames	☐	☐	☑	☐
Old-fashioned quilted bed covers	☐	☑	☐	☐
Modern abstract art	☐	☐	☑	☐
Chrome and glass furniture	☐	☑	☐	☐
Dark mahogany wood	☑	☐	☐	☐
Purple painted walls	☐	☐	☑	☐
Pine country-style tables	☐	☐	☑	☐
Metal CD racks	☐	☐	☑	☐
'60s Sputnik kitchen clocks	☐	☑	☐	☐
Plaid upholstery	☐	☐	☑	☐
English landscape oil paintings	☑	☐	☐	☐

Congratulations, you just voiced some of your style preferences. In order to develop your style, you must become *opinionated*—about what you see, touch, smell, hear, and especially how you feel. Every time you glance in a store window, enter someone's house, flip through a magazine, or watch the TV, quietly ask yourself if you like how things have been designed, arranged, and organized, and if what you see evokes a positive emotional response. Is your style traditional, eclectic, urban contemporary, American country, Danish modern, '50s chic, or another? Discovering what brings you personal joy and fulfillment is how you find out. Owning that style is a stepping-stone to becoming more yourself—a huge leap toward deeper personal growth.

Test-Drive Your Style

As you work through this section, make informal visits to furniture showrooms and the lighting and housewares sections of your local department stores. Sit on the furniture. Rub your hands across upholstery or wood finishes. Test-drive the pullout beds inside those convertible sofas you expect your guests to sleep on. Try out lighting fixtures. Bring a magazine along and try to read under floor lamps. Think about shape, color, texture, and practicality. Check the maximum wattage of lighting fixtures—40-watt bulbs don't throw off enough light to read by. Sit at dinettes and check for sharp edges where your elbows will rest.

Browsing without the purpose of buying frees your imagination to really see what is appealing and what is not, without the urgency of need. Ask yourself which items you found most practical and which ones you were most drawn to: Were they plush? Tailored? Conservative? Futuristic? Formal? Scotchgarded? Unveiling your taste should be fun, so approach it like a game. Enjoy yourself. If you're unfamiliar with design styles, ask the sales personnel whether an item is traditional, contemporary, or some other style. That way you can put an identifier on your taste. You might also want to casually browse some items you'll need for the COMING ATTRACTIONS in your life just to get ideas. But this is mainly a *style* exercise. When you return, create a section called MY STYLE in your *Emotional House Design Binder* and add any brochures, notes, or pictures you collected during your mission.

Doggie in the Window—A Game of Taste and Decision

This is a game you can play anytime you go shopping. Take a friend and go window-shopping. Pick a place you can browse without interference. It doesn't matter what kind of store it is, as long as it relates to the home in some way. It can be plumbing fixtures, vases, china, decorative items, junk shops, whatever you might find in your house.

GAME RULES

You have to make a choice and decide on one thing you would buy from that window, display rack, or display table. Do not actually buy the item—this is a decision game, not a transaction game—but compel yourself to pick one thing you would take home if you had to. You *have* to pick something even if you hate everything you see. On the other hand, if you love everything, you must narrow your choice down to just one. Force yourself to commit—one thing and one thing only. Then make your case about the choice. Both you and your window-shopping buddy have to cop to the reasons why you chose the item and ruled the others out.

Was it the color, style, function, or craftsmanship? Does it remind you of something or someone? Or are pink ballerina lampshades your secret guilty pleasure? Explain. Listen to your friend's choices, as well. It not only ups the hilarity, but it will help you expand your ability to see why other choices get made, informing your own decision and helping you see the beauty in things you hadn't considered. After you've made your cases, move on to the next window.

This is a great exercise to discover what you love and why, and a good way to get you in the habit of making choices. Children love these sorts of games, but if you play with a child, make certain they know up front that no purchases will be made. With children, sometimes it's better to play this one when the store is closed. When you get home, pin yourself down on your process.

Were the things you picked:

- ☐ Extravagant
- ☐ Classic

- ☐ Minimalist
- ☐ Whimsical

- ☐ Functional
- ☐ Other

Were they:

- ☐ Sleek
- ☐ Rustic

- ☐ Kitsch
- ☐ Ornate

- ☐ Colorful
- ☐ Shiny

Did they make you feel:

- ☐ Thoughtful
- ☐ Nostalgic

- ☐ Silly
- ☐ Sweet

- ☐ Special
- ☐ Powerful

What else can you say about the things you picked? Did you notice a pattern, a theme, a color palette, or some other similarities among the things you were drawn to? Keep a record of what you're learning about your taste in the MY STYLE section of your *Emotional House Design Binder*.

The Four Senses

Engage your senses. When it comes to personal style, include sight, sound, touch, and smell. If you do nothing else but let your senses lead you, you'll awaken yourself into your experience and make a house that looks, sounds, smells, and feels pleasant. That's not too shabby. Pick a favorite room from your childhood that you remember loving. It could be a place in your childhood home, or in the home of a grandparent, aunt, friend, or another.

What did it smell like?   _____

What kinds of sounds did you hear inside?   _____

What colors were prominent in it?   _____

What textures did you touch in it?   _____

If any, what patterns were repeated inside?   _____

What kind of furnishings did it contain?   _____

Was it spacious or crowded?   _____

Wonderful *textures* like suede or rough stone underfoot, *aromas* of fresh flowers, the homey smell of a baked apple pie, *sounds* of snappy jazz on the CD player or a small water fountain burbling on your desk, *sights* of rich color on the walls, stimulating art, meaningful memorabilia, glistening tile, and polished antiques help shape your experience in your home and make it an Emotional House. Sense-memories are so powerful and lasting that manufacturers are now addressing this with powerful products too. Procter & Gamble offers Scentstories fragrance disks for the home that "play" on CD-like machines and reproduce complex fragrances with names such as "Relaxing in the Hammock" and "Exploring a Mountain Trail." Indeed the sensory revolution is blazing new trails. Start making positive sense-memories for yourself, too.

The Fundamentals of Style

There are various aspects to selecting a style that fits you: shape, pattern, texture, color, and more. So let's start out with one of the basics—shape.

Shape = Function

Shape equals function. Which is to say, the form of something determines its task. A straight, stiff-backed chair will provide a rigid seating area—a very useful seating choice if you don't want someone to stay long ... and a poor choice if you want the opposite. An antique chair with delicate lines and disposition also provides a fine seating area, but indicates a formality about the use and dictates your behavior around it. Conversely, a tumble of plump pillows spread across the floor provides ample seating but might invite a raucous sprawl of physical activity.

When you choose furnishings, it's important to consider your daily routine, the requirements of your circumstances, and your personality. Take all three things into consideration. Your personality (formal/casual, etc.) will decide if it's delicate antiques or a more casual contemporary style that suits you. But your daily routine and your requirements all contribute to your style choice as well: Do you have children, pets, messy roommates, work projects in the house? These will also impact your style choices.

Choose the shape you find most pleasing:

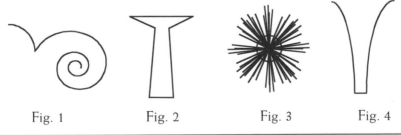

| Fig. 1 | Fig. 2 | Fig. 3 | Fig. 4 |

Did you find it difficult to pick just one, or did you home in immediately on your selection? If you chose Figure 1, you might lean toward the clawed table footings of European antiques or perhaps the plush overstuffed sofas of shabby chic. If you chose Figure 2, you may prefer furnishings with cleaner tailored lines, like Scandinavian contemporary or perhaps early American. Figure 3 aficionados are more experimental; you may enjoy retro or futuristic décor. If Figure 4 was your choice, then possibly eclectic, French provincial, or traditional fare appeals more to you. Now let's look at patterns.

Pattern = Continuity

Which patterns are you naturally drawn to?

- ❑ Checks
- ☑ Stripes
- ❑ Plaids

- ❑ Polka dots
- ❑ Paisleys
- ❑ Flowers

- ❑ Scenic prints
- ❑ Geometrics
- ☑ Solids only

Coordinating patterns is a way to bring continuity to your environment. The eye relaxes with a repetition of form, color, or arrangement. There's a sense of relationship. It's a detail worth taking into consideration when deciding on your décor.

For instance, if you chose checks as your favorite pattern, you can repeat that pattern by establishing groups of square-shaped objects throughout the room. (Group things in odd numbers, not even numbers for a more interesting look.) You can also repeat a color from a dominant drape or upholstery fabric in your throw cushions, ottomans, or accessories as a way of establishing pattern around a room.

If flowered patterns were your choice, you might add fresh flowers or scenic art pieces to enhance the connection between the flowered upholstery of your sofa and the nature that inspired it. In the kitchen, chair seat cushions, tablecloths, napkins, and window treatments can be repeated to coordinate a look. If overdone, any pattern can seem too deliberate and feel forced, but adding simple splashes of the same fabric, pattern, or color throughout the room can be calming and elicit a sense of balance. Even a set of table napkins or placemats can do the trick.

Texture = Depth

Textures add depth to your experience in each room—from sofas to floors to drapes and linens. Like smells, textures are often intertwined with memories; they connect with the old brain and appeal to our tactile nature, which comes from deep within and has much to do with what makes us feel at home. The smooth shell of a plastic chair engages your playful side. Mottled leaded glass on a kitchen cabinet draws out your homey nature. The complexity of a silky Persian rug excites your secret inner sophisticate. Icy chrome and leather appeal to your ambitious strategist. Consider in which rooms these textures are most appropriate and inject them throughout your home to add interest to your environment and to broaden what touches your inner sense of peace or strength.

If you're not sure about what textures to use, just think back over your life and identify some textures that have made an impression on you, for better or worse. Did your grandmother's velvet scarf make you feel safe? Was it soft, scratchy, nubbly? How did it make you feel?

Look at the list of textures below and write any emotional responses you may have to them. For example—Rough/Scratchy: *Burlap curtains make me feel down-home and rebellious.* Or *sandy-textured walls make me feel unwelcome.*

Soft/Smooth: _____

Rough/Scratchy: _____

Plush/Cushiony: _____

Silky/Slippery: _____

Hard/Shiny: _____

Are there some textures you definitely want to bring into your environment and others you want to keep out? Consider this when choosing flooring, fabrics, and furniture.

Color = Mood

Bringing color into your home is a natural way to create a mood and affect yours. Color can be dramatic, soothing, lighthearted, bold, subdued, sensual, and more. Moods are often described in terms of temperature. He's hot tempered. She's coldhearted. And colors, too, are described as either warm or cool, based on their wavelength. Take a look at the color wheel of primary and secondary colors. Warm colors are on one side of the color wheel: red, orange, and yellow. Cool colors are on the opposite side: green, blue, and violet.

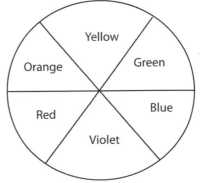

Choosing cool colors as your favorites doesn't mean you're a cold person, it just means those colors are pleasing to your eye and you resonate with those hues. Maybe you're a person who "runs hot," whose life is intense and harried. You may need the cooler colors to feel balanced and calm. Similarly, there may be times in your life when things are slower or tedious and you might want to inject warmer hues into your home to get the motor running again. Look around at the colors in the room you are in right now.

What is the dominant color in this room? _____

Does the color resonate an ambience? _____

How do you feel looking at this color? _____

Does it stimulate the work you are doing on your Emotional House? _____

Try to imagine the walls painted an entirely different color: a deep blue, hunter green, chocolate brown, dark red, or shocking pink. Does the mood of the room change at all for you? It's fairly easy to see the importance of color in a room when you think of adding strong colors, but all color has an effect of some kind. Discovering which colors you lean toward is an important aspect of your personal style, and you will get a chance to do that in the pages ahead. Of course, what you think is heavenly at age twelve could be hideous at fifty, so be prepared for some changes. Our experiences and other influences transform our styles over the years and our homes' color palettes should change accordingly.

Theme = Story

One way to engage your imagination and quell unfulfilled dreams is to reproduce characteristics of a place, thing, or activity you love in your home. Designing around a theme—whether it's color: the blue room; an activity: the reading room; a favorite vacation haunt: a Parisian bistro kitchen; or even a memory like an afternoon with your father: the fishing boat bookcase in the den—can transport you right into the experience. It can be like taking a daily holiday in your own home.

Answer these questions:

What are your two favorite cities? _____

Where did you spend your favorite vacation? _____

What two spots do you love to go to (beach/library etc.)? _____

What is a favorite memory? _____

Which color is most prevalent in your closet? _____

What activities do you most enjoy? _____

Make a note of these possible theme ideas for your rooms in the MY STYLE section of your *Emotional House Design Binder*.

DESIGNING AROUND A THEME

An associate, who works long hours and entertains for business, enjoys the South Pacific so intensely that he transformed his house, from entryway to garage, into a tropical oasis. On his porch, he wrapped his exterior lighting fixtures with bamboo and placed potted tropical plants that heralded the theme ahead. Inside his living room, the scheme begins to take hold with a complete Polynesian grass bar and comfortable lounging chairs arranged around the room, all lit with amusing hula lighting fixtures.

By the time you get to the backyard pool, you're ensconced in an inviting grotto of natural rock and cascading waters, bordered by verdant gardens of ferns, palms, flowering hibiscus, and banana trees. The pathways are natural stone, lit by gas-powered bamboo torches. Even his exterior garage gate is constructed out of large bamboo trunks with a wooden tiki mask as the door pull. This extravagance may be a little too much for many people, but for him, it's truly a South Pacific haven in the heart of Los Angeles's smoggy San Fernando Valley.

Choosing a place you love to be and instilling your home environment with some of those characteristics is a wonderful way to bring that flight of the imagination to mind and subdue the restless feeling of being boxed into a life of responsibility and obligation.

Feathering Your Nest

Now that you have the basics, it's a good point in your process to get more specific. Let's go on a field trip. You are going on the hunt for your *personal* collection—the colors, patterns, textures, and looks you absolutely love.

The Collection Phase

In this exercise you will be picking up fabric swatches, paint chips, tile samples, and brochures for wood flooring, stains, and molding that you *absolutely love*. You will find these trips very useful—just as designers do when they are prepping for a new collection. They go exploring and so will you. Your first mission is a trip to your local hardware or home improvement store.

CHIP DIP—ADVENTURES IN PAINT

First stop is the paint department. Head to the paint chip display and pick up all the paint color chips that you respond to favorably. There's no other agenda—deciding what *colors* you like is the whole aim, not which color you are going to paint a specific room.

When you return, place your samples in the MY STYLE section of your *Emotional House Design Binder*. We'll work more with them later.

WALLFLOWER POWER—DÉCOR IN A ROLL

Next, visit the wallpaper section. The same drill applies here. Grab samples you like. You may have to page through several display books to peruse samples. Some stores give swatches, while others do not. But if you see one you like, jot down the info and check it out on the Internet. If you own a color printer, you may be able to print out a copy later.

When you return, add them to the MY STYLE section of your *Emotional House Design Binder*. A lot of people have strong opinions about wallpaper because of the loud patterns  and bold colors that dominated in the past. But wallpaper is back and many specialty types are now available, like the Anaglypta and Lincrusta brands with embossed, decorative 3-D friezes, wainscoting, and border relief patterns. These are designed to be painted, and they add a whole new dimension to your walls or ceilings by giving the impression of costly plaster effects—at a fraction of the cost.

If you don't have samples to staple onto pages in the MY STYLE section of your *Emotional House Design Binder*, write down the patterns you like that you want to revisit later.

WOOD AND TILE FILE—
FINDING YOUR FLOOR, MOLDING YOUR FUTURE

Don't forget the tile and flooring aisles. You may only get brochures for flooring, but if you are industrious enough, you can take a trip to an outlet that specializes in molding and flooring or tile and granite. Many will let you go away with practical samples of half a dozen tiles or a board or two.

Natural hardwood flooring has had a comeback in the last fifteen years, as have granite kitchen countertops. Make yourself identify your preferences: Do you prefer the muted or the colorful, the simple or the ornate, light or dark woods, polished inlays or grainy finishes?

When searching through the rows and collections of stone, granite, and tile, ask yourself: Do glistening, white ceramic tiles in your bathroom make you feel clean and renewed, or does the mottled finish of natural stone conjure fantasies of bathing in a secret cove?

You may already know what you like or have noticed something in someone else's home you admired. The offerings are many—and only a trip to a ceramic tile, stone, and marble yard or flooring shop will give you answers. While there, check out baseboard molding designs and the carved wood architectural features as well. You can enhance your mantel, door entrances, and walls with these inexpensive but fabulous carved wood features—many for under ten bucks.

You may be years away from even thinking about flooring, countertop, or tiling jobs, but go and explore these elements anyway. You are developing your personal design style and informing your senses. Browse and have fun, but bring home only the things that you like, even if you don't think you could actually live with a giant flowery print as wallpaper.

SWATCH WATCH—FABULOUS FABRICS

Now, it's on to a top-notch fabric store or outlet. Check one out in your phone book—and start with the good stuff, so you know what's out there. Don't be afraid of expensive designer's collections—you are browsing, *not* buying. If approached by store proprietors, tell them you're redoing your house and looking for selection samples. They'll be more than happy to assist by cutting a few fabric swatches for you to take home. But try not to let their opinions influence you too much; they're not living in your skin. Look around first, find what you like, and only then ask for a sample. Perhaps you've always bought your furniture and draperies off the floor of a department store or have never been in a fabric store before. Your world is about to open up! Curtains, comforters, and table linens can all be made to your specifications and furniture can be recovered to coordinate with your personal taste.

Pay attention to each fabric's texture. You want materials that feel soothing to your skin and measure up to your wear-and-tear factors and issues like sensitivities or allergies. Some wonderfully colorful fabrics have come onto the market, but many are synthetics that could rub you the wrong way during extended use. You are creating an Emotional House, a healing environment—and as you'll find out later, comfort always trumps fashion. Remember, this season's trends are not what you're looking for; you're looking for *your* style. You don't have to commit to any of these now or later. Like the paint chips and wallpaper samples, these fabric swatches are simply going in your *Emotional House Design Binder* arsenal to help you get a feeling for what you love.

After you've assembled your whole collection, put all your samples on a table in front of you and read on…

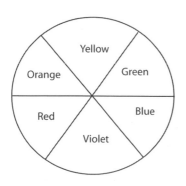

The Color Wheel

Back to the color wheel of primary and secondary colors. Separate your paint chips, tiles, fabrics, and wallpaper into piles that most closely match the color categories on the left.

Red, yellow, and blue are primary colors. They comprise the basis for all color. Orange, green, and violet are secondary colors. They are colors made by combining two primary colors together. There is a third category, called tertiary colors, made from a combination of primary and secondary colors. Most likely, the majority of your paint chips and fabric samples fall somewhere into that last category—reddish orange or bluish green for example. But for now, try to match your chips to the section on the color wheel that seems most dominant.

Which colors are your most prominent selections? Write down the number of paint chips you have in each group.

Red # _____	Blue # _____	Green # _____
Yellow # _____	Orange # _____	Violet # _____

Write these down in your MY STYLE pages. Now that you've realized which colors you actually lean toward, you've discovered an important aspect of your personal style palette. It will be easier to create color schemes and design combinations from this palette and imbue your home with the colors and textures you love.

Your personal style arsenal is really starting to grow now. In the Color Therapy section of House Rule #11: All White Is Not Right (chapter 19), you'll begin creating color schemes that benefit your spirit, disposition, and lifestyle, but for now, pop your samples back into your *Emotional House Design Binder*.

Magazine Motifs—Becoming Your Own Clipping Service

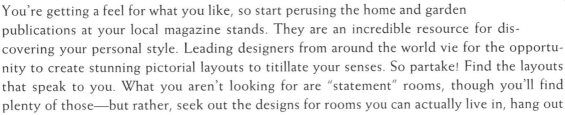

You're getting a feel for what you like, so start perusing the home and garden publications at your local magazine stands. They are an incredible resource for discovering your personal style. Leading designers from around the world vie for the opportunity to create stunning pictorial layouts to titillate your senses. So partake! Find the layouts that speak to you. What you aren't looking for are "statement" rooms, though you'll find plenty of those—but rather, seek out the designs for rooms you can actually live in, hang out in, and be comforted by. Keep your daily routine in mind. Are white plush carpets realistic when you live with children or animals, or will you have to exclude the people and creatures you love to be with, in your own home? There is something so sad when a pet is relegated to the basement because the homeowner has created a pet-unfriendly environment. You'll want to consider all of these issues when you think of your personal style. Create an INSPIRATION section in your *Emotional House Design Binder* and staple any pictures you love there.

> **DON'T JUST WAIT . . . INVESTIGATE!**
>
> While waiting in line at the grocery checkout, pick up a home décor magazine and quickly leaf through it. If a pictorial layout catches your eye, buy the magazine. Clip out the page and add it to the INSPIRATION section of your *Emotional House Design Binder.*

Bringing It All Together

What you've been doing throughout this chapter is gathering an understanding of your style by looking at the elements in your home in terms of shape, color, pattern, texture, and theme. They all have the ability to produce a feeling or a mood or reflect a personality. All are part of your personal overall taste. The days of flipping through all those weekend newspaper ads in search of the cheapest furniture sales are over. You can still look for bargains for your Emotional House, but you want to do more than just fill your home with random sticks of furniture. You want to create a look—*your look*—it's your Point Of View. That means employing a discerning eye when making your selections. The next time you go to purchase furnishings or decide on a new look, take all of these characteristics into consideration. And don't forget about the other extras that perk everything up—sound and scent. These will help you bring your POV together in a uniformly pleasing, yet wonderfully stimulating manner.

HOUSE JOURNAL

Much of what you've learned about your style is no doubt hard to verbalize and pin down into absolute categories. So, before we leave this chapter, let's engage your right brain and try something nonverbal. Draw a simple form or shape that can represent the essence of your style. It could be a circle, a triangle, a free-form shape, or a rose; you can draw it with a ruler or with your eyes closed. This is not about your ability to draw, it's about your ability to surrender to your imagination. Keep it simple and if you don't get it, don't worry.

Next, add color to the drawing. Use as many colors as you want.

Complete this paragraph: I now realize that style means something different from trendy; it's not the same as fashion, and my own style is much clearer to me. When it comes to style, my home and I _____

PART II

YOUR FOUNDATION

❧{ 8 }❧

House Rules

Afoundation of cement, rebar, and gravel is the underpinning structural support for any building, without which the structure will crumble. Likewise, the foundation of an Emotional House needs boundaries, comfort, beauty, cleanliness, order, efficiency, and proper room function to support a good life. You can create that sturdy base by following some basic rules for the vital components of an Emotional House—true for every house and for every room.

HOUSE RULES

RULE #1: Live in Your Whole House

RULE #2: Keep It Clean

RULE #3: Comfort: First and Foremost

RULE #4: Lifestyle Dictates Design Style

RULE #5: A Show House Is No House

RULE #6: A Place for Everything and Everything in Its Place

RULE #7: Art Is Smart

RULE #8: Set Boundaries for Room Use

RULE #9: If It's Broke, Fix It

RULE #10: The Divine Is in the Details

RULE #11: All White Is Not Right

RULE #12: A Room of One's Own for Everyone—Including Pets

❧{ 9 }❧

HOUSE RULE #1
Live in Your Whole House

Spend time in each room in your house every day to generate a more balanced life.

Live in your whole house. This is the very first principle for one reason: It's the most important. Everything in an Emotional House rests on this principle. To live your complete life—in harmony with your heart's desires and your mind's potential, in balance with your needs for work, play, and love, in support of your needs and the needs of your significant others, and without stress—you need to live in your whole self. To live in your whole self, you need to live in your whole house. Homes are designed with all your needs in mind, and once you start cutting yourself off from certain areas of your house, you're cutting yourself off from parts of your self. Why would you do that?

We've discovered a lot of people live in only one room. For some it's the kitchen, for some the den, and for many it's their bedroom. They pile everything into that one room: eating, hanging out, reading, making things, working on things, talking on the phone, sleeping. What's wrong with it? Why is "Live in Your Whole House" the number one rule? Because:

Each Room Serves a Practical and an Emotional Function

While the Four Cornerstones define an Emotional House, every room in your house also serves two purposes: a practical function and an emotional function. Each room addresses basic needs like food, water, and shelter, as well as deeper, more personal needs like camaraderie, serenity, and intimacy. You could even call them your *soul's* needs. When a cozy, warm kitchen smells like the roast sizzling in the oven, an apple pie cooling in the window, and coffee brewing on the counter, the function of that room for the ten-year-old doing homework at the table is going in deeper than just getting fed. For the mom or dad who has created a kitchen that can serve both these functions so well, it's much more about nurturing the being of that kid than about putting food in his or her mouth.

Psychologist Abraham Maslow's (1943) time-honored Hierarchy of Needs states that we have survival needs of food, water, shelter, and security at the base; these evolve into emotional needs for privacy, belonging to something greater than ourselves, recognition of our talents and work, and the creative expression of our deepest selves. Or in simpler terms: to be free, to connect, to contribute, and to grow. An Emotional House provides a basis for *all* these needs to be met room by room.

SURVIVAL NEEDS	SOUL NEEDS
food	to be free
water	to connect
shelter	to contribute
security	to grow

Every room has both a practical function and an emotional function. These functions affect your daily life of survival and also your soul needs above that. When either the practical function or the emotional function of a room doesn't work, then the room doesn't serve your needs. For example, if there is an empty space where a living room should be, then how can the occupants "commune" with others in an appropriate way? Perhaps they have chosen not to live in any kind of community, at least not in the deepest part of themselves (in their own home) or not in the light and easy part of themselves (in the public space of a family room). But a living room is a sort of "tribal council," a gathering place for one's inner circle—where your need to connect is fulfilled at home.

But why would someone avoid this or any room? The answer is usually in an underlying emotional disappointment that has caused a disconnect from the need—in this case, disengaging from the need to connect. Perhaps it was a traumatic event or just an ongoing, imperceptible experience of neglect that suppressed the emotional need, but the end result is a lack of wholeness.

By addressing each room in the home with your basic and emotional needs in mind, you take steps to heal those disconnects, establish new practices, create new routines, and benefit from the proper utilization of your space. The effort creates a more balanced, satisfying life.

What's more, if you've displaced a survival need—like the need for food—into an emotional need—like the need for connection—it's in the wrong place; and that's where you need healing. This may show up as an eating disorder, for example. By the same token, if you are fixated on an emotional need, like the quest for freedom, you might eventually threaten your survival needs by not acquiring the resources you need to provide your food and shelter. On the other hand, an obsession with security can become so stifling that it cuts you off from your need for liberty, tying you to a job or a home that limits your personal growth. By structuring your home to properly meet all your needs, you correct and balance the way you function in your life.

Are all these needs met in your life to your satisfaction?

- ❑ Food & water
- ❑ Shelter
- ❑ Security
- ❑ Health

- ❑ To be free
- ❑ To connect
- ❑ To contribute
- ❑ To grow

If any of these needs are getting too much attention or too little attention in your life, they will likely show up as HOTSPOTS in your home. For instance, if your whole life is all about serving others' needs and not your own (an over-emphasis on contribution), you might find your bedroom cluttered with toys, your living and dining rooms a depot for volunteer organizations, and no space of your own to relax and refill—necessary components in developing personal growth. Contribution is a valuable gift to others, but you must stay in *balance* to be able to continue your efforts, and that means taking care of yourself first. Make a note in your HOUSE JOURNAL of your needs that aren't being met.

Your Home Is the Starting Point for Getting Your Needs Met

How do you translate an intangible emotional need into a tangible application in your home? Let's take the essential emotional need "to be free" as an example. This means that you require a personal space of liberty—a private haven in your home where you are allowed to

be and do as you wish, undisturbed, like Dad's classic den. Having a space of your own is a crucial component in creating a stress-free environment and when others support you by respecting that space, your cornerstones are being covered. There is one caveat: If your "personal territory" is located in a common area, it must not impinge on the emotional or practical needs of others. You simply can't appropriate the entire living room for your personal workshop if there isn't another area like an extra family room that allows fellowship for everyone else. You can, however, divide the room and make it multifunctional.

That's how design can effect change in your life and meet your emotional—or soul—needs, as well as respecting the needs of others. Creating an Emotional House that works means every room should function correctly.

THE PRACTICAL AND EMOTIONAL FUNCTIONS
OF EACH ROOM OF YOUR HOME

ROOM	PRACTICAL FUNCTION	EMOTIONAL FUNCTION
FOYER (The Gate)	Transition	Equalizing
KITCHEN (The Hearth)	Physical Sustenance	Nurturance
LIVING ROOM (The Tribal Council)	Fellowship & Entertainment	Camaraderie
DINING ROOM (The Round Table)	Communion	Bonding
BEDROOM (The Sanctuary)	Sleep, Solitude & Sex	Intimacy
BATHROOM (Temple Bath)	Purification	Reverence
HOME OFFICE (Central Records)	Business of the Family	Value & Accountability
BASEMENT/GARAGE (The Keep)	Storage	Remembrance
KIDS' ROOMS (The Fort)	Nursery/Hideout	Becoming
STUDIO/WORKSHOP (Labor & Delivery Room)	Creative Arts	Expression
GARDEN/PATIO (Eden)	Cultivation & Harvesting	Serenity
RECREATION ROOM (Playhouse)	Gaming/Fitness/Fun	Release
LAUNDRY ROOM (The River)	Washing & Folding	New Beginnings

You'll learn more about these specific functions in Part III when you work on each room individually. But even if you don't have all the rooms listed in the Functions Table above, you need all these functions in your life, so you must find ways to fit them in. In chapter 2, you were asked what part of your life was *really* working for you right now. Does that aspect of your life fit into the correct room it was designed for? For example, if you said your work was going tremendously well and your personal sense of value and accountability was extremely high, but now notice that the Functions Table says the bedroom is designed for intimacy (not marketing and making deals), you might discover one source of your problems with intimacy. Perhaps you haven't made room for that emotional function in your life, or you are shielding yourself from it with work. The solution isn't to stop working, but rather to move the work to an appropriate and equally comforting location, so you can enrich your life with intimacy as well.

In the HOUSE PLAN section of your *Emotional House Design Binder*, jot down all of the emotional or practical functions that your home currently does not satisfy. When you get to House Rule #8: Set Boundaries for Room Use (chapter 16), you'll learn how to multipurpose rooms to include these.

What Part Are You Leaving Out?

The question we ask clients who have malfunctioning, imbalanced, inharmonious, or stressful rooms is this: What needs help here? Is it a decorating quandary, a lack of adaptation to a life change? A problem with traffic or workflow? Or is there a hidden, deeper reason, like an unpleasant memory or an issue with something that's present in the room?

Understanding how each space meets an emotional need, it's useful to look back to something that happened in your life that caused you to disengage from that area. One woman discovered that she hated the dishes her mother had passed on to her and it was keeping her out of her own kitchen. In these inconspicuous plates lay unspeakable memories of childhood dinners filled with criticism—not a *nurturing* experience. The moment she replaced her dishes she began using her kitchen and never had to swallow those bad memories with her bacon and eggs again.

We all have parts of ourselves that are stunted, neglected, injured, disowned, or abandoned—it's part of life to experience setbacks and to make choices; sometimes you have to go back and pick up missing pieces along the way; other times new parts of you burst forth like a seedling through newly watered soil, catching you without enough space to accommodate the sapling within. You will find all these parts of you in your home. Leaving any parts out will cause your cornerstones (harmony, balance, support, and a stress-free environment) to crumble.

Go through the Functions Table, and check the rooms against your EMOTIONAL ROLLER COASTER ROOMS that you listed in your HOUSE JOURNAL. Jot down the practical and emotional functions beside each of those rooms. There is a connection there; can you see it? If you weren't gently nurtured emotionally in childhood—if a well-meaning parent thought nurturance was relentless "constructive criticism"—you may have developed an indefinable guilt, a burning resentment, support issues, an eating disorder, or a poor relationship to food. No wonder the kitchen has become an EMOTIONAL ROLLER COASTER ROOM for you. The kitchen is where nurturance, both physical and emotional, begins. Your life will improve as you work on this room, learn to nurture yourself in new ways to heal those wounds, and move your life into your whole house.

HOUSE JOURNAL

Now you are on your way to creating a house that you can really *live* in. The important thing is that you do live in it! Practice by using this exercise: Write for five minutes in your HOUSE JOURNAL every day while sitting in a different room, until you have written from all of the rooms of your house. Use the Functions Table to remind yourself of the practical and emotional functions of the room before you begin. Then write about how this room really functions and how this room truly affects your emotions. If you have ideas about what you'd like to do to fix the room, make a note of it while it's fresh in your mind and jot it down in the HOUSE PLAN section of your *Emotional House Design Binder*.

HOUSE RULE # 2
Keep It Clean

Vacuum and dust the house, clean the toilet, and launder the sheets once a week. Wash all dishes and wipe down counters every day to maintain a healthy home.

There's a reason housekeeping chores are the first thing new recruits in the army are required to do at boot camp. They teach honor and respect for yourself and your things, even when you have little, and they teach respect and how to behave responsibly toward others—the one bunking next to you, as well as the whole unit—all with simple, direct actions and clear, observable tasks. Making your environment clean is not a humiliating activity as so many people these days seem to think. It is the most basic act of taking care of yourself.

Even if you can't find time to redecorate your living room, redo your kitchen, or retile your bathroom, you can do wonders just by keeping your house clean. A clean house sparkles even when it needs to be painted. And with cleanliness comes a freshened environment full of potential for new experiences.

If you farm out some of these duties to full-time staff, pay them well. They are the caretakers of your history, your treasures, and your hopes and dreams, which are spread throughout your house, arranged into little stories if you are awake to them. You're entrusting them with everything you own, including extensive handling of all your possessions when dusting, cleaning, and putting things away.

But unless you can afford a full-time house staff, you can't get away with no cleaning responsibilities at all. Dishes need to be done and food preparation needs to be cleaned up and put away, if nothing else. If you can't even do that, then you're living on that borderline of disregard and disrespect. Whether this insolence is originating from you or aimed at you from your household members, it results in violating all four cornerstones: dirt and mess are stressful; leaving the responsibility for cleaning them up to someone else doesn't support anyone; and as messes develop into filth, any feeling of harmony is coughed, gagged, or itched away—sapping the balance from your living conditions and, ultimately, your relationships. Why would anyone bring stress, disease, and disrespect in to live with you like a family member? Cleaning is not only the easiest (and least costly) design element to take on, it can be shared by everyone in the family—from the tiniest toddler to the most recalcitrant teenager.

> **TIP** Make vacuuming all your floors a whole lot easier by installing a cord management system that lifts cables and cords off the floor and fastens them at baseboard level. Master Caster Cord Away (J style) and 3M's Cord Clips are effective solutions.

Three Cleaning Absolutes (They're Health Issues!)

Regarding cleaning, there are three absolute musts:

1. **The bathroom must *always* be clean.**
    Leaving a dirty, smelly bathroom for others to use—whether it's in your house or someone else's—is more than just disgustingly poor manners; it's making a haven for staph infection, hepatitis, mold, mildew, and so on. But a clean bathroom shows a high-minded love for the bodies and spirits of all who enter.

2. **Dishes, kitchen counters, and stovetops must be washed and wiped down whenever soiled, and spotless *every night* before you go to bed.**
    Food remnants invite vermin of all varieties—from microorganisms like salmonella to insects and rodents. In addition, it's always better to walk into a clean kitchen that is ready for you to prepare a little something than to find yourself in a dirty one with no available space to create sustenance. And in the morning, it's truly like facing a fresh new day that wants something good for you.

3. **Sheets must be washed once a week in hot water.**
    The oils and flaky dead skin sloughed off while you sleep are what dust mites live for, and they will proliferate in dirty sheets. You might not be able to see these microscopic monsters, but if you don't have allergies already, you will likely

develop them if you make a habit of sleeping in piles of them. You can't get away from them entirely, because they're everywhere; however, you can sanitize your sheets weekly in detergent and hot water, killing the mites off and keeping their offspring's food supply low.

TIP Tackle big cleaning jobs in small, manageable steps. Start with the easiest task. Work in 15-minute increments. Put on mood music.

These clean conditions are the mark of a civilized home, and the baseline of an Emotional House. But you can go deeper. You can D.U.S.T.

The D.U.S.T. Principle

The D.U.S.T. principle is the whole reason for this House Rule having the #2 position. Cleaning is basic, but this straightforward method uses the letters D.U.S.T. to help you unearth the emotional issues that have moved in with you. This is called "spiritual house-cleaning." You clean out your feelings while cleaning your house, removing the negatives and leaving you with a clean slate around which to build your Emotional House. So, let's go.

D: Discover the Dirt

Check back to your HOTSPOTS again and review the rooms you listed as embarrassments and the ones that have a junk and filth problem. We call these "ghetto" areas because they have apparently been abandoned, as have the parts of you they represent. Name the rooms here:

_____ _____ _____

_____ _____ _____

Sometimes dirt is emotional in nature and not easily seen. This debris frequently shows up in overly spotless rooms or rooms you avoid or rarely use. Name the rooms you identified in your HOTSPOTS as being furnished, but never used. Add in any other rooms that are meticulously spotless to this list:

_____ _____ _____

These rooms aren't functioning properly, either—even the "perfect," spotless ones.

There's one last room you'll include in this exercise—your least favorite room. You named this room in chapter 2, at the very beginning of this program. Write it down here.

_____.

Remember, you tried to identify what made you feel "icky" in this room. If you didn't know then, now's your chance to find out. Your task is to go through each of your rooms and dust thoroughly and unhurriedly. Even if you have a regular cleaning service, dust every single item that you have made a home for inside these rooms and reflect on it as you do.

Take mental note of the items that make you feel great and set aside *any* items that give you that icky feeling or bring up a bad memory. Make a list of those items here.

_____ _____ _____

_____ _____ _____

U: Understand the Use and Meaning of the Room

You have your D.U.S.T. yuck list now—the rooms that are a problem and things inside those rooms that are a problem. Go back and review the practical and emotional functions for these rooms on the Functions Table in chapter 9. Understanding the proper use of the room helps you connect the dots to the issues you're struggling with in your life. This step is the *key* to making your home a source of support in your life. The rooms that are filthy tell you what part of your life wants attention. For example: If your bedroom is a disaster of filth and clutter, you may have trouble with intimacy or developing a sanctuary for yourself. If your dining room is overly perfect, you may have an issue with loosening up enough to allow for bonding with others. Perfectionists will resist this thinking, but perfectionism in itself screams out the need to control every little detail. And beneath that control need is the fear that if things aren't controlled, unwanted emotions will bubble to the surface. The purpose of the D.U.S.T. exercise is to do exactly that: Bring these issues to the light of day so healing can begin and an Emotional House can result. Now move on to the next step.

S: Screen the Stories

Get out your HOUSE JOURNAL. It's time to screen your stories. All of your stories are hidden in your house—the good ones and the bad ones. But those nasty demons you've tried to sweep under the rug have done nothing but give you a lumpy floor. Instead of trying to hide the emotional refuse that is festering with rot, bring it to light and stick it in the compost bin to be transformed into useful fertilizer that will grow your future better self.

Anyone who has ever cleaned out a closet or packed to move knows that handling your *things* floods you with the stories of your life. And your HOTSPOT areas are full of them.

Georgie, who you'll remember lived in her bedroom and was having difficulty finding a partner, had a beautifully designed and spotless living room that she avoided like the plague because art pieces given to her by an old boyfriend who broke her heart were displayed there prominently. That emotional dirt needs removing, too. Screen your possessions for stories that make you feel bad—whether they are things that hold bad memories or gifts from people you simply don't like.

An old friend of one of the authors, Jill, had a hideous vase on her stair landing given to her as a wedding gift by an obnoxious relative. Every time she climbed the stairs to her bedroom, she said aloud, "I hate that vase. I bet she bought that ugly thing on purpose." This went on for years, yet Jill resisted getting rid of it because it was a wedding gift, commemorating an occasion that was happy and important to her. This resistance to releasing a toxic gift meant every climb up the stairs to her marriage bed was marred by a slap in the face. It came to the point where she dreaded going upstairs at all. Think of the impact that could have.

Other possessions will give you a positive experience with good memories and hopes that are still alive, and things you are grateful for (a paperweight your favorite uncle gave you when your story was picked for the school newspaper … are you still writing?).

Check out the rooms and the items you noted above and write down in your HOUSE JOURNAL why they feel good or nasty when you check in with yourself. What are your stories for these rooms and what needs to be retired to the compost bin?

T: Take Action with Both Trash and Treasure

Now you know the problems; you understand the room functions; and you've discovered the stories. It's time to take action. If something trashes your spirit, toss it. Maybe it's a set of dishes that reminds you of inharmonious and stressful dinners with unhappy parents. Dump them like the woman mentioned earlier did and get a starter set from a discount store—it's worth the twenty bucks to eat off a clean slate. You don't have to live with things you dislike or keep things from people you don't want to think about, even if they are occasion gifts, like the wedding vase. Purge those items. Destroy them in a personal cleansing ceremony. Or resell them at a yard sale. Your trash will be another's treasure. If you can't throw whatever it is out just yet, box it up and put it away with a good label—Yuck Box—for revisiting later.

More important, if you have things that seem to uplift your very being, that make you feel good, then you should treat them like treasures—their sparkle lends strength. Like your favorite chair: Take an action beyond dusting, vacuuming, or cleaning it—polish it, recover it, or add a new throw over the arm and add to the treasure of it. Or that paperweight from your uncle—move it to a creative workspace for inspiration.

A clean house is more likely to be a stress-free environment than a dirty one. You can relax. You feel like someone's taking care of you. That means it gives you support too.

Cleaning at the level of "spiritual housecleaning" fills your house with harmony and light. This does not mean your home needs to be sterile. A sterile house is starving for life, not life sustaining. Strike a balance here and you've got another brick in the foundation of your Emotional House.

> ## RULE OF THUMB
> If an item in your home doesn't make you feel good, eliminate it!

What You Allow Becomes Standard

"Well, haven't *they* just let themselves go?" You've thought it before, maybe even said it. Maybe you've even thought it of your own house. On some level, you know how it happens: What you allowed became acceptable. This is how a dirty house becomes unlivable without your seeing it coming. It's how a pile of dirty clothes or wet towels dropped onto the bathroom floor becomes a normal sight. If not addressed immediately, it quickly becomes the standard.

This is why you need to know what your own standards are and to learn how to communicate them to your children as well as the adults in the house and persuade them to participate with you in maintaining those standards. You might want to have this conversation with your own inner child as well—the part that resists adult behavior and lacks personal responsibility. This will not happen in one conversation or multiple screaming arguments or through bribes. It comes from guidance (showing them how), supervision (assigning the task and overseeing it), and demanding compliance (with consequences). When you don't enforce standards, you either live in filth that is below your standard of cleanliness, causing stress and disrespect to flourish, or you become a screaming nag … also not a very harmonious picture.

A family of four requires four people to maintain an Emotional House. One of them alone (i.e., the *mother*) cannot do it all by herself. As in the story of the Little Red Hen, everyone must participate if they want to live in harmony and balance. Nonetheless, one of the most common questions we get is, "How do I get my husband (boyfriend, girlfriend, roommate) to help?" Admittedly, it is difficult to "train" another adult to maintain standards that he or she doesn't share. In the following pages, we present some suggestions and systems, such as the Chore Chart, that might make it easier to state your case and get your mate to share in the work of household maintenance. Another very good solution can be found in House Rule #12: A Room of One's Own for Everyone (chapter 20), which allows others in the house to keep a private area just as they like without interference. When a person has a private space where their messes can run rampant, they are often more open to respecting the common areas of the home, where that is not an option. Perhaps creating that private space can be the reward for holding the standard.

One thing is sure: Marriages that comprise a partnership, working together to maintain shared values and standards, are happier and stronger on all four counts: *harmony, balance, support,* and a *stress-free environment.* It's the ones where mutual respect is not honored that are fraught with conflict. Try to move toward the center and develop your standard together. Start with middle ground, where you both agree, then move on from there. When you hit rough ground, don't keep going till you get a flat tire. Take brief detours on common ground again before you venture back to the rocky road.

Getting Kids to Help

It's best to start when they're young with required chores—not for money, but for being on the planet. But if you missed that opportunity, it's never too late. When changing conditions make what was once the habit suddenly unacceptable, you must explain that to older children and then assign them daily chores. One can vacuum the living room and hallways once a week. Another can keep the porcelains and fixtures clean and sparkly in the bathroom. They can alternate doing the dishes and sweeping the kitchen floor every night. These are common areas, and common responsibilities for children as well as adults. Dividing chores amongst the members of the family and setting a day for them to be done is fair and ordinary for many families. Kids and adults can also all be responsible for putting their own clothes in the laundry and stripping their sheets Saturday mornings.

If, at the end of the day, household chores have not been completed, there must be consequences. Period. Parents can use their completion as a bargaining chip for privileges that family-membership also presents—movie money, dessert, going on a sleepover, borrowing the car, getting time on the computer. If you skimp on the consequences, the foundation of the Emotional House cannot hold.

The Chore Chart:
Creating a Cleaning System for Your *New* Standard

A clean house needs more than lip service. Develop a system in just three steps.

1. Take an hour to decide on the future standard of how your home will be kept.

2. Call a family meeting (or a house meeting if you live with room-mates) and set down the standard. Remain open to discussion, but assert your desires until an agreement is reached.

3. Create a schedule of weekly tasks and post them on the fridge or a memo board for all to see. Your CHORE CHART will keep the new standard alive for everyone.

This isn't just a "make your bed and mow the lawn" chore list. Laundry needs to be included. Anybody over twelve is perfectly capable of doing their own wash. A family of four has at least ten loads of wash a week. Do it two loads at a time throughout the week—Saturdays are taken with linens. Chart out who does their laundry when.

SAMPLE CHORE CHART

TASK	DAILY	WEEKLY	ASSIGNED TO
Dishes and kitchen counters	Wash & clear before bed		Mon–Tues: Daughter Wed–Thurs: Son Fri–Sun: Dad & Mom
Floors and furniture		Vacuum & dust Saturday	Daughter
Toilet and sink	Everyone keeps toilet free of waste	Scrub with cleanser Saturday	Son
Bed linens		Strip & wash on Saturday	Kids & Dad strip the beds. Mom washes.

We are all too busy and our physiological systems too stressed to have to handle the toxicity of poor health conditions in our own homes—and that's what an unclean home sets up. If bugs, germs, and bacteria like your house, it's not healthy for humans. Good house-keeping is required to keep everyone well and in balance and stress-free. It is part of respecting yourself to live in a healthy, clean environment. So keep it clean.

❊{ 11 }❊

HOUSE RULE #3
Comfort: First and Foremost

Introduce at least two "purely for comfort" items in every room in your home.

Comfort is not just one piece of business in your design—it's got majority share. Because home is where you love yourself up, and that's all about comfort. Comfortable seating, comfortable beds, comfortable environment, atmosphere, and manner. Social rapport develops more easily in a comfortable setting and tempers are more readily calmed. Comfort adds harmony to style, balance to form, support to your weary bones, and a stress-free environment to buffer you from the burdens you shoulder. That's why it's among the top three rules.

Which of your rooms did you identify as causing you the most stress and discomfort on your HOTSPOTS page? Addressing the comfort factors there is a must.

Physical Comfort

The Perfect Chair

Every home should have a perfect chair. Is yours a comfortable haven that holds you for hours without back pain? Do your feet touch the floor and is your back against the chair's back when you sit? Your elbows and forearms should rest lightly on the arms of any chair, hanging loose and relaxed from your shoulders. There should be no strain in your wrists, elbows, or neck. Neither should there be strain in your mid-back, hips, knees, or heels. Unless everything about you is "average," you might feel some strain when sitting in the "average" chair.

Size Matters

For whatever reason—could it be that most furniture designers are still male—most chairs are designed for the "average-sized male." In fact, everything from your car seat to your bed, from your sofa to the height of your kitchen countertops is generally sized for the convenience of the 5'9" man. Were it only so that this guy did all the cooking and washing up. Unfortunately, his centrality means a world of discomfort for the rest of us—whether shorter or taller, wider or more petite. Back problems caused by ill-fitting chairs are responsible for a high percentage of work-related absences.

Designers of the Aeron chair, a nearly perfect task chair made by Herman Miller, say, "A chair should fit the body like a piece of clothing. People shouldn't be required to 'wear' chairs that are too big or too small." We agree—your furniture should feel at least as good as your sweats do. Do you know how to try on a chair?

Measuring Yourself for the Perfect Chair

Measure the length of your thigh from your behind to the back of your knees while sitting down. The chair seat (seat pan) should never hit the backs of your knees. Next, measure from your kneecaps to the floor. That's the maximum height—from seat pan to floor—you'll want for a chair, in order to have your feet reach the floor comfortably. Unfortunately, this is a tall order for petite individuals who almost always need to take advantage of footstools and lumbar supports when seated, as well as for tall folks whose knees can pop up so high they block their view to the TV. Why is all this important? Two words: your spine. A proper chair can be the difference between a healthy spine and a compressed disk. Yes, comfortable furniture isn't just about function and beauty, it's also a health issue.

In the MY STYLE section in your *Emotional House Design Binder*, write down your measurements. Take them with you when you go shopping for new chairs. If you do only one thing for your Emotional House, give yourself a perfect chair and a good light. It will serve many masters, offering you a quiet retreat, a reading area, and a beautiful focal point that says "You are welcome here."

Physical Comfort as a Health Issue

Chair measurements aren't the only health considerations in an Emotional House. There's a design trend that could pose a health hazard for many sensitive individuals: fabric-covered walls and upholstered headboards. It's true they look fabulous and seem so cozy, but they are fraught with health risks for people with asthma, allergies, and other respiratory illnesses. Fabric is a magnet for dust and a haven for allergy-causing dust mites, which thrive in mattresses and bedding, along with other airborne allergens and germs. While you can clean your bedding in hot water to combat these problems, you can't clean an upholstered headboard or a fabric-covered wall. Vacuuming helps a little, but nonporous surfaces you can actually dust and sponge down are best, at least in the bedroom. It's something to consider if you have wall-to-wall carpeting as well. There's nothing comfy about not being able to breathe.

The Bed

In an average lifetime you spend approximately twenty-four years in bed, a third of your life, so

the bed is an important piece of furniture for you and your children. And a revolution has taken place in bed design. Manufacturers now offer beds with adjustable and varying firmness for two separate sleepers. If you like a soft mattress and your partner likes a firm one, you can buy spring mattresses made-to-order to accommodate both needs, or air mattresses that have an internal mechanism that allows on-the-fly adjustments. There are also the open-celled, breathable foam beds, like the Swedish Tempur-Pedic system, that are made of pressure-relieving material. The Tempur-Pedic was originally developed by NASA for space travel and forms to the natural shape of your body and spine, but is quite costly. Whatever you choose, always budget for and invest in a top-of-the-line bed. You spend a lot of time there and a good sleep will rejuvenate your energy resources and emotional health.

The Linens

Go organic when it comes to linens. Chemically untreated, 100% cotton or linen sheets with a high thread count breathe well, do not pill, last a very long time, and soften with age.

Good sheets are expensive, but worth every penny—they never rub you the wrong way like those made of synthetic products, such as polyester, do. Get sheets with a thread count of 300 or higher if you can. When an all-cotton sheet claims to be no-iron, it's been chemically treated. Popping an untreated sheet right out of the dryer and onto the bed will give you that freshly-ironed feel, and you won't have to sleep with unnecessary chemicals.

The Air You Breathe

The Environmental Protection Agency now estimates that indoor air pollution may be up to five times higher than outdoor. There's been a dramatic increase in asthma and allergies in the last few years—dust, mold, smoke, pet dander, dust mites, and pollen being the major offenders. One solution is a HEPA air filter. And every household should own at least one.

HEPA stands for high-efficiency particulate air filter; these are available everywhere, including drugstores, at very reasonable prices. HEPAs filter out 99.97% of particulate matter as small as .03 microns. Place one in each bedroom and change the filters every six months. The filter cartridges are expensive, so buy several whenever they're on sale.

Resale Comfort?

Recently, kitchen designers have noticed a marked increase in requests for differing heights of kitchen and bathroom countertops. Right behind bad backs from poor seating lies the problem of sore shoulders from doing dishes in high sinks or preparing meals at high counters.

While some homeowners still worry about adjusting the height of counters and breaking "the height standard," the Emotional House Program condones the option. Make a home that works for *you*, not one that works for the day of resale. Most people live in their homes for an average of five years, so why opt for 260 weeks of discomfort? When installing new cupboards, getting countertops three or four inches lower could be the difference between years of strain and an utterly joyful culinary life. Unless your kitchen counter height is at knee level, most potential buyers won't notice if it's a few inches lower; besides, many new homeowners will redo the kitchen to their own tastes anyway. For those who still balk at the idea, a small footstool near the sink and a lower prep table can help.

Aging Adults and Comfort

Design issues come to the forefront as you age. "Universal design," which means building for all ages, is a new concept starting to take hold, and forward-thinking homeowners in middle age are installing grab bars and age-assisting appliances in anticipation of future physical challenges, when upgrading their bathrooms. Some seniors still consider condos as a smart trade-down from that rambling two-story home, however, and while leaving behind the familiar can be stressful at first, maintenance companies who handle the heavy lifting and elevators that replace steep steps bring relief. Selling a long-term home that has risen dramatically in value can also be a terrific life enhancement in senior years. Emotional Houses come in all sizes, and once you've had one, the feeling can be reproduced anywhere.

Aging adults also need to consider the materials they will live with in the future. Slippery granite bathrooms and ceramic and stone kitchen floors, while hot on the market, are fatiguing to less-than-stable legs and downright dangerous to brittle bones and arthritic hips. Consider wood and carpet if you're thinking long-term, except in areas with special requirements like an entryway from the pool. All stairways require railings, and grab bars should also be installed in baths and showers, along with traction mats to reduce slick surfaces. For the kitchen, there is a plethora of new easy-grip appliances for arthritic hands. For the bedroom, a whole new kind of warming blanket has hit the market. These are not at all like the bulky wired heating blankets of old. The new warming blankets can be washed in the washing machine and have microfilaments so thin you barely notice them. They also have timers so you can heat up the bed before you get in—a great feature at any age.

Emotional Comfort

Emotional comfort means your home should be filled with relationships that are in harmony. If it isn't, you need to take action by getting therapy or making changes to correct those issues. Your life should be balanced by ensuring that the rooms of your home fulfill their correct emotional and practical functions. But you need to live in your house, so nothing should be too perfect. Your life goals and physical activities should receive support through the cooperation and assistance of your cohabitants as well as the practical design. And your daily experience should be relatively stress-free of interpersonal conflict and the hassles that disorganization creates. Oftentimes comfort simply comes from what isn't there.

The Positives of Negative Space

Artists understand the positive aspects of negative space, which are blank or white areas in artwork, deliberately unpainted to allow the eye to rest and see more clearly what the artist wants viewers to focus on. It's the same for the home. When there are areas left clear and free of objects, one visually and emotionally rests in the quietude of that absence. Conversely, when every nook and cranny is crammed to the gills, the busyness inside causes the eye to gloss over the mass in order to shield itself from being overwhelmed. And there's nothing comforting about that.

The Japanese culture, home of minimalist Zen Buddhism, takes the concept of negative space to the level of art in homes. Strategically-placed artworks and furnishings set within bare expanses offer decidedly peaceful environments that calm and center the mind.

Emi Ayarza, who owns Emi's Treasures, a small antique store in North Hollywood, works in an environment packed from floor to ceiling with relics and treasures. Emi's home couldn't be more different, a minimalist paradise with wide corridors of space to "charge through," as she puts it, without hindrance. For Emi, creating good movement flow results in emotional comfort. On the face of it, it appears that Emi needs relief from her congested work environment. But in telling her story, she recounts a childhood of persistently bruised shins caused by unfortunate furniture placement. Filled with enormous energy, she was always forced to slow down and assume a deliberate and judicious comportment to keep from getting hurt.

Today, while she can stand slowing down at work, her home must comfortably support her natural pace, with all pathways kept wide and clear. Emi claims that if she has to make even the tiniest adjustment in her freedom of movement, the furniture gets moved. Negative space exudes harmony for Emi.

Comfort Crutches

Embracing a comforting memory from your childhood by bringing items that remind you of it into your adult home honors your personal history while bringing you emotional comfort. Think of these as "comfort crutches." Just as hospital crutches prop you up when you're injured, these comfort crutches at home hoist your spirits when you're feeling low. Every life has its tough periods, and that's when comfort crutches are especially helpful.

If, as a small child, you had a tradition of having tea in fragile little teacups with your beloved grandmother, as one of the authors had, starting your own collection of fine china

teacups will offer you the emotional comfort of a cup with Grandma every time you settle down with a hot pot of tea. If it was the Southern tradition of iced lemonade on the veranda that holds sweet memories for you, acquiring a tall glass pitcher and lemonade glasses may do the same trick. Hanging a porch swing, displaying copies of old photographs, or throwing a regular game night with your friends can keep comfort moments alive.

So often in adulthood the business of living keeps us from the simple pleasures of life. There's a quiet joy in reexperiencing soothing childhood experiences even now. Remember to claim your history, treasure the ways you felt soothed when you were little, and celebrate yourself in this way. A Comfort Crutch is good medicine for the soul.

HOUSE JOURNAL

What good memories from your past have you brought into your house? Walk around with your journal and identify them. Then move any Comfort Crutches you have to the room in which they would best support you (review the Functions Table on page 65 in chapter 9 for emotional functions to see where they'd best fit). If you can't find any emotional comfort items, write about your current sources of comfort and make a list of some positive memories from your childhood that you want to bring into your adult home. Make a note in the HOUSE PLAN section of your *Emotional House Design Binder* of the particular rooms you want these to be in.

HOUSE RULE #4
Lifestyle Dictates Design Style

*Stop fighting your own habits. Accept who you are and create a
living environment that fits.*

Your lifestyle—your daily routines and activities—needs to dictate the way your home is laid out and designed. If it doesn't, then your home becomes a critical parent constantly scolding you for how you are. Daily life in such a home feels like irresolvable conflict. That's not an Emotional House, that's an overwrought trap. But if you view your everyday life issues as a simple design problem rather than a lifestyle problem, solutions abound.

Back in Part I, Your Blueprint, you identified specific logistics and problems in your home and daily life. This exercise informed you about the current and future requirements of your life to help you prioritize your design plan. The problems you uncovered point to the design choices you need to make as solutions.

Your lifestyle and goals come before your designer's great ideas, before your friends' opinions of what's cool or your parents' beliefs about what's correct. That concept is at the core of this whole program. For example: Farmhouses look like farmhouses because the life mission of farming dictates very specific needs. Farmhouses virtually always have a mudroom of some kind where people can kick off boots and dirty work clothes, thereby containing the debris from barns and the fields. Farmers don't deny the fact that they get dirty—they acknowledge it and provide workable solutions. The lifestyle dictates the design style.

By the same token, if you have young kids or big dogs, your home will develop a certain look that you can either facilitate with style and hardy furnishings, or succumb to in chaos with closed-off and restricted rooms. Remember House Rule #1: Live in Your Whole House. A closed-off room closes off an emotional as well as a practical need. If athletes live in your house, there are going to be gym bags, wet towels, and smelly clothes and shoes to deal with. You can pretend this is a temporary condition and let these items take over the foyer, living room, bathroom, or bedroom and have your whole home smelling like a locker room, or you can design a place and a process for handling them.

You need to designate a hallway, a corner, or a closet for cubby cubes, a storage bench, and hooks to accommodate the slosh, mess, and dirt that goes along with the joys that dogs, athletes, and kids of all sorts and ages generate. Otherwise you'll still get the mess, but not the joy.

Which of these lifestyle choices are creating design stressors at the moment?

❑	Spouse	❑	Athletics
❑	Children	❑	Gardening
❑	Pets	❑	Entertaining at home
❑	Roommates	❑	Travel
❑	Hobbies	❑	Gaming
❑	Home business	❑	Other _____

The HOTSPOTS you identified in chapter 2 are probably linked to some of these activities. Your home is already screaming out its problem areas to you. Spots of clutter, disorganization, grime, or total abandonment are the pointers to a design style that is not meeting your lifestyle. Just as are those worried little faces that know they are offending somehow, but don't exactly know how to change it—what to do, where to go, how to clean up properly, or the places where it's okay to play or stow things. Pick one of the HOTSPOTS in your home that you consider disorganized, congested, embarrassing, or as being filled with junk, and try this exercise below.

Four Steps to Addressing Lifestyle Conflicts

STEP ONE: CORRECT ROOM FUNCTION. The Functions Table in House Rule #1 (chapter 9), defines correct room usage. If your dining room has become a storage facility, you've lost an important location for bonding with the family. If your fitness equipment is in the living room, how can you have fellowship with your extended community? Move anything that doesn't belong in this room out.

STEP TWO: ADD STORAGE. If the clutter that's occurring belongs in this room—paper buildup in a home office for instance—add storage like bins and filing cabinets as a solution.

STEP THREE: CHANGE OR ADD FURNISHINGS. If this doesn't satisfy the problem, the furnishings may be too formal (or too loose) to meet your current lifestyle. You may be living with a décor style that you have outgrown or transformed beyond, especially if you run a business from the home and meet clients there for whom you need to make an impression. Perhaps your furniture requires just too much care for your active lifestyle. Change it, Scotchgard it, or add slipcovers and tablecloths.

STEP FOUR: PARTITION ROOMS FOR ADDITIONAL FUNCTIONS. Finally, if you don't have space for all the functions you need to service your lifestyle, you will have to *multifunction* your rooms (a task you'll learn more about in chapter 16 on House Rule #8 about setting boundaries).

Once you've put those design priorities in proper perspective, you might find your life improves even as your house becomes lovelier.

One Woman's Design and Lifestyle Story

While one person might change their design style to fit their best lifestyle, the danger is in having a design style that *determines* your lifestyle. A personal associate who wants very much to find a permanent mate and start a family has been touting this goal for over a decade. This young executive is a high-powered, successful, and attractive woman with a terrific job, high income, and great overall presentation. She wears the latest styles, and she's well-groomed, trim, and always looks fabulous. Her intellect and sense of humor are considerable. On first blush, she is a great catch. But move in a little closer, and her personal issues begin to show signs.

Despite her affluence, she cries poor when it comes to her home. Even though she can afford to buy an upscale condo, she is adamant about living frugally in a tiny sublet on a dark street. While she spares no expense in her physical appearance, her undecorated apartment doesn't reflect who she is or what kind of life she wants … in fact, it tells her potential suitors to turn and run.

Like it or not, potential mates are shopping for someone with a skill for nesting. That is what a partnership is all about: creating a nest together. And there is nothing more attractive about a person than their home.

In insisting on what is a crippling frugality, this wonderful woman has relegated herself to a lifestyle that tells herself and the whole world that she is a transient, that she isn't entitled to a home, and that she isn't even heading in that direction. She has sentenced herself to a life that she doesn't feel like she's chosen and that she wouldn't choose. And yet she *has* chosen it by the way she insists upon living in her home. Her design has determined her lifestyle, not the reverse. If she changed her home, she would change her life. And you can too.

Lifestyle Reality Check

What are the realities of your lifestyle based on your routine, habits, activities, and responsibilities, and those of the other occupants? Think in broad strokes. For example, you might say: I'm a single mother with two kids in day care. I like to jog every morning. I have a full-time job, plus I run a small business out of my home on weekends. One of my children has special needs and requires constant supervision. I can't afford to go out much, so I entertain on the cheap at home with microwave popcorn on DVD movie nights. I always take one evening off for myself each week to soak in the tub and read, no matter what.

_____

Now you try:

The reality of my lifestyle is, I am a _____

_____

_____

How I live now is _____

_____

_____

Now that I think of the realities of my lifestyle, my ideal setup should be more like _____

_____

_____

1. What kind of furniture do you need?

    ❏ Casual   ❏ Formal   ❏ Designer

2. **What kind of furniture do you have?**

   ☐ Casual ☐ Formal ☐ Designer

3. **What color rug would be appropriate?**

   ☐ Dark ☐ Light ☐ Patterned

4. **What color rug do you currently have?**

   ☐ Dark ☐ Light ☐ Patterned

Approach each design element in this manner: Look at your lifestyle and decide what kind of furniture you need first. Then, review what kind you actually own. You'll quickly see how things match up and why problems get started. It's a great reality check. Make notes about the style of décor you need to fit your lifestyle in the MY STYLE section of your *Emotional House Design Binder*. You'll use them when you start working on Part III, Your House. What do you need? Where do you start? Check all the following that apply:

1. **You entertain:**

   ☐ Frequently ☐ Occasionally ☐ Never

If you entertain a lot, you will need dishes that can stand up to the size and liveliness of your guest list. You will need a service area for beverages and snacks that leaves the main chef/caterer in peace to cook and serve. Someone with this lifestyle would benefit from a wet bar with a fridge in the main entertaining area and roomy sideboards in the dining room.

2. **You enjoy cooking:**

   ☐ A lot ☐ Sometimes ☐ Never

If you cook a lot, you need a stocked pantry, a baker's rack, a good fridge with a freezer that works, and a pot rack to accommodate quick retrieval of cooking pans. Even tiny kitchens can have a pantry. Check out cupboard-based pantry options available in stores now. But even if you don't cook at all, you still have a need for support and a kitchen that nurtures you. Focus your design solutions instead on a good-sized microwave for heating up boxed, frozen, and canned foods and a toaster/broiler for frozen precooked foods.

3. You take pleasure in:

☐ Reading   ☐ Surfing the Net

☐ Sewing   ☐ Listening to music

☐ Writing   ☐ Watching TV & DVDs

☐ Hobbies   ☐ Playing video games

☐ Woodworking   ☐ Playing an instrument

These lifestyle choices all require proper space, seating, equipment, and lighting to do them justice. They can each impinge on the needs and rights of other members of the household, so the solution lies in multifunctioning rooms that support like-minded activities. The aim is always not to interfere with practical and emotional functions. See House Rule #8: Set Boundaries for Room Use (chapter 16) for instructions on how to create multifunctional spaces.

4. You have a hard time throwing things away:

☐ Always   ☐ Sometimes   ☐ Never

Attractive storage bins and a top-notch labeling machine are mandatory tools for collectors. Determining what will be displayed in a place of honor, like on a table or bookshelf, and what will be stored in a well-labeled bin for future retrieval is the way to transform the mess into workable packets of possessions. If collecting is your natural style (some call you pack rats), you need to address that personality trait with design solutions instead of fighting who you are. It's hard to change people, but implementing a design solution can facilitate a stress-free environment. See chapter 14, House Rule #6: A Place for Everything and Everything in Its Place, for more tips.

5. You exercise at home:

   ❑ Regularly   ❑ Occasionally   ❑ Never

If your living room is overrun with exercise equipment, it's a gym, not a room of fellowship. But designers are starting to work with America's desire to exercise inside with new and attractive multifunctional equipment. Hidden Grove Furniture has an ingenious armoire design that combines a home office with a treadmill and weight bench that easily hides away after use. (See the Resources section for more information.) Considering your routine, habits, and the realities of your *actual* lifestyle will help you define a design style that offers more support.

The HOTSPOT you identified as the least functional space in your house is a good place to start. Write down three lifestyle or design style solutions you can think of right now for this space. And add these ideas to your HOUSE PLAN section.

1. _____

2. _____

3. _____

❦{ 13 }❧

HOUSE RULE #5
A Show House Is No House

Use it or lose it.

You've seen those stunning magazine layouts of perfect homes. Glistening marble stair-
cases, imported silk drapes, and perfectly lit sculptures on revolving pedestals. Who
wouldn't drool over them? They are gorgeous masterpieces of design and beauty—but
would they allow for the complications of your particular life?

A home should be the place where you can come in, kick off your shoes, lean back, and
heave a satisfying sigh of relief from the storm of the world. It shouldn't be a place where a
formal set of prescribed behaviors is constantly required.

A Show House vs. an Emotional House

It's no good to build your house to someone else's specifications, and it's never right to decorate your home to impress someone who doesn't live there. It's simple: If your house is "for
show" and not for living, it will be fine for showing, but not for living in. Any shelter that's
not meeting *all* of your particular emotional needs will cut you off from those needs, and you
will not feel sheltered by it. You might as well live in a display window. That's how comfortable you will be in your own home. Think of your cornerstones: While a show house may
present the illusion of harmony and balance, the very unreality of a show house means it can

never be a stress-free environment. And what kind of support requires you to draw a curtain of phoniness around yourself?

Throughout this book, you have been identifying and defining the *real* you. The logistics and issues of your environment and life, as well as your personal tastes and style, all need to be addressed to create a home that meets your real needs and your true character, thereby enhancing your optimum experience of living. We all have a persona that we present for show from time to time. However, we hope the questions and opportunities for reflection that we've offered will help you separate the real you from the *show* you. A great presentation is always loveliest when it is centered in authenticity.

One Client's Story

While planning a kitchen renovation, a client happened upon an ultramodern model kitchen at a high-end Beverly Hills shop. The sleek design was arresting, complemented by soaring floor-to-ceiling cabinets that had breathtaking visual impact. This was undoubtedly a "power" kitchen. Anyone who entered this room would get the immediate impression that the owner was a person of substance with significant resources and a commanding sense of style.

The client ruminated for some time over the design and the equally imposing price. She liked the impression it gave, but after considering whether this was a room where she would want to hang out, bake, sit on a stool with her husband having dessert, or converse with her best friend over a glass of wine, she quickly realized that it was not an inviting space for her real life. Beyond the stunning design, it was cold, distant, and fashioned purely for impact, with only cursory functionality. She wanted a kitchen that was homey, comfortable, and friendly. This kitchen would be none of those things. Getting in touch with who she really was—*not who she wanted people to think she was*—made her realize that a country kitchen was more to her liking. The kitchen is the room of nurturance, where your senses and body are fed; a power kitchen didn't do that for her.

"Get up so I can make the bed"

Having a show mentality is akin to insisting on perfection: both make for a very unpleasant life. This order, "Get up so I can make the bed," was heard every weekend by the family of a woman whose entire house was for show. Her husband wasn't allowed to walk through the living room (he might leave footprints on the carpet), children weren't allowed to cook in the kitchen (they made a mess), and no one was ever allowed to sleep past 7 A.M. (beds can't be made as long as someone is in them). When you live like this, it's not long before everyone feels disconnected from their home. And in this case, the result was a distant marriage and alienated children.

The truth is, no one really enjoys being in a show house and no one is warmed or impressed by it. Visitors don't feel comfortable. They don't know where they can sit or set down a drink or whether they can keep their shoes on or must leave them at the door. If your intention is to isolate and drive others away, you won't be moving toward creating an Emotional House. Living leaves evidence of itself. A show home is no home because it doesn't allow for living.

Review the rooms you identified as "furnished, but never used" on your HOTSPOT list. Then look back at the Functions Table in chapter 9 (page 65) and determine if all your emotional and practical needs are currently being met by your home. Is every soul need being met? Is there a special place in your home to grow personally? Make a note now in your HOUSE PLAN to transform this show room into a useful space that meets a missing need.

HOUSE RULE #6
A Place for Everything and Everything in Its Place

*Determine a home base for all belongings and add storage
containers wherever clutter gathers.*

As Denver home organizer Bev Sullivan says, "Everything needs a home, even if that home is in the trash." Organization has become one of the biggest problems in the modern-day home. The Information Age is in full swing and we are submerged beneath a mountain of paper. Women are no longer full-time CEOs of the household, always available to sort, wash up, and clear away. A huge percentage of families are now headed by single parents, and our increasingly consumer-oriented way of life has stuffed our homes to the gills with new products. Ten years ago, DVDs weren't the standard, home theater systems were only for the wealthy, and fitness rooms were usually made up of a single bench press in the garage. Builders weren't prepared for the flood of small businesses that would be run from the home, the high-volume communication centers that would emerge, and the growing electronic demands of busy households. It's no wonder the home front is suffering!

Organizing and storage systems are the answer. Begin by increasing shelving and cabinetry and organizing vertically, utilizing that priceless empty wall space everywhere in the home. In the kitchen, add pot racks to ceilings to empty out cupboards and make space for pantry organizers.

Assigning a place for everything you bring into the house and returning everything to its place after you've used it is a no-brainer. Clutter is not only stressful and a huge waste of time and anxiety, it's just plain dumb to be bogged down for a half hour every day searching for your keys because you haven't made a place for them to be or you didn't put them there when you came home. Conversely, an attractively organized room lessens stress and contributes to that good feeling you identified in your favorite room in chapter 1, What Is an Emotional House?

If you can afford one, professional organizers are a godsend. But if you can't, set aside just two weekends to:

1. Assess your clutter and identify the HOTSPOTS.

2. Purchase storage bins and put them into action at those sites.

Stores now offer attractive bins and baskets in every shape, size, and design—from plastic to wicker. Buy more than you need at the outset so empty containers are available that coordinate with your overall presentation. You will begin your journey of turning your whole home around. Your final destination is an efficient, stress-free environment—an important Emotional House cornerstone. Organization begets organization. And preplanning for useful organization and storage elements will help keep task areas clean and functional and prevent them from becoming Clutter Central. Always place an attractive centerpiece or bowl of fruit or flowers on your dining table to hold the place for future dining use. Empty surfaces seem to just call out to junk mail and random papers as the location to pile up.

Tips and Strategies for Organizing

Two Rules of Thumb

1. **Where things go has to make sense for how they are used.**
   Hang your keys on a hook by the door, or set them in a bowl wherever you naturally want to set your stuff down.

2. **The hall closet cannot be *the* place for everything.**
   If you can't look in it and see everything that's there, it's become a place where things get lost, not where they are kept.

The Organizer's Answer to Disorder: Hooks, Boxes, Bins, and Baskets

These things typically do not have a proper home:

PAPER—Mail, magazines, catalogs, reports, etc., constantly flow into the house and grow into piles and piles and piles …

CLOTHING—It's constantly coming off: coats, hats, mittens, shoes, and clothes too clean to launder, but too dirty to put away

KITCHEN AND HOUSEHOLD TOOLS—Everything from dishes to food to appliances to batteries tends to be everywhere or nowhere in particular

KIDS' AND PETS' TOYS—Watch where you step; these are downright hazardous

> Store it,
> don't stuff it.

Name four organizational problems that have become emotional or practical issues for you. For example, are you frustrated that you are often late for work or engagements because you can't find things? Are bills not getting paid by their due dates because they're getting lost in the paper shuffle?

1. _____

2. _____

3. _____

4. _____

Changing habits is a long-term effort that takes time and discipline, but getting relief now isn't impossible. Start by looking at where you have a tendency to dump things and create an interim workable solution by placing a container for these items in that spot. Next develop a workflow system for handling them. We'll begin with the greatest offender: paper.

Creating a Workflow System

Mail

THE PROBLEM: Important mail and bills get lost in the excess of junk mail. Prior to the modern era, people had a secretary in their front hall where the mail was handled—a tidy little slant-top stationer's desk with different-sized slots that held stationery and the family ledger. We need those again, though updated to accommodate a laptop computer and a cell phone charger. If you can find one, buy it (the Bombay Company offers several terrific varieties).

THE SOLUTION: Create your own easy mailroom system with three bins. Label them PURGE, PERUSE, and PAY.

PURGE • PERUSE • PAY

The 3 Ps of your mail system will help you sort out the junk mail. Assemble your bins in tiers: PURGE on the bottom, PERUSE in the middle, PAY on the top. Sort mail daily as follows:

PURGE. You are not required to read all the junk mail and catalogs sent you. File junk mail in the bottom bin, tier three, for recycling.

PERUSE. Letters, notices, announcements, subscriptions, and your favorite catalogs that are worth spending time on go in the middle or second tier of your bin system.

PAY. Bills go to the top tier. The best thing is to pay them at once and document the payment (date, amount, check number) on the bill stub, in your check register, and in a software accounting program if you use one. If you don't pay bills immediately, review your top tier once a week and put those coming due at the head of the pile. Credit card companies make a fortune on late fees that often run $25 per offense or higher. *Never* throw away your bills, credit card statements, or any bank account information without shredding first. Identity theft is on the rise. Keep all bills, payment documentation, and receipts in this bin until you can transfer them to your properly categorized tax files. (Financial records must be retained for seven years. The IRS requires it.)

OUTGOING MAIL CLIPS	EXTRA STAMPS
Hang a clip at the door for outgoing mail. When you write a bill, walk it to the clip. When you leave the house, take the bills with you to post.	Buy two rolls and put one at the door in a small box and one at your desk where you write out your bills. It's always good to have a backup.

Okay, you have everything in containers now, but you haven't had the time to read everything yet and your bins are starting to reach capacity. On trash day, toss the bottom bin (the junk mail). It is a freeing act, and you will immediately experience your reward: The Relief Factor. Next sort through your second-tier bin. Some things will stay, but you might find that quite a few items end up in the bottom recycling bin for next week's disposal.

Clothing

Clothing is a clutter problem because it's perpetually in one of five stages:

- Soiled, requiring laundering or dry-cleaning

- Freshly laundered, waiting to be put away or ironed

- Damaged, requiring repair

- Stored in drawers or closets, awaiting selection

- Clothes too clean to launder, but too dirty to put away

You need to address all five of these stages with storage solutions or you will have clothing clutter and constant questions like "Is this clean or dirty? Is this for the cleaners or are you wearing this tomorrow?" and so on.

> ## PURGE CLOSETS ANNUALLY
>
> Fashions change drastically, so those size 8 jeans you're saving for your weight loss will probably be out of style when you get there. Shopping for new clothes should be the reward for any major weight change, anyway.

The solution to clothing clutter? A laundry workflow system that addresses the way you actually live and the areas clothing gathers in your house.

What you'll need:

- Multiple stackable laundry baskets of the same size and style.

- Decorative secondary baskets for common clothing clutter areas.

- A wardrobe valet (or set of hooks) to hold clothes ready to be worn.

HOW TO SET UP YOUR LAUNDRY SYSTEM

1. In the laundry room (or a closet), create three shelves for baskets. Label them SOILED, CLEAN, and NEEDS REPAIR. Put your stackable baskets in here.

2. In your HOTSPOT areas around the house, where clothing collects, place your decorative baskets, which you will empty into your soiled laundry basket on laundry day.

3. In your bedroom, place your wardrobe valet, a piece of functional furniture that doesn't give the impression of clutter, like clothing laid across chairs can.

4. In your closet, hang your clothing on identically styled hangers (wood are recommended). The visually pleasing hangers won't bunch up or hang at odd levels—easing both slide and selection.

5. In your dresser drawers, store like items or color-matched items together.

When all five stages of clothing have a home, it's easier to manage the family's wardrobe without having a daily drama about getting dressed or arguments about who's a slob. It might not be you having the drama; it might be your husband or daughter, which is why the system needs to be shared by everyone.

UNIFORM HANGERS

Choose a hanger style you like and purchase enough for your entire wardrobe plus 10% for new clothing purchases. They'll hang in a uniform line, won't bunch up, and will make it easier to sort through your clothes.

CLOSET CLEARANCE

Divide closets into three sections.

1. Clothes worn currently
2. Clothes unworn for one year.
3. Clothes unworn for two years.

Everything else goes in the donation bin. Change over your sections every New Year's Day.

Eyeglasses

Buy a good pair of glasses and then get additional pairs in cheap frames or extra readers from the drugstore. Place them in uniform containers in each room so you'll have visual access everywhere you go. Some optical stores will give you a deal on multiple pairs, and frankly, it's always good to have a second pair in your car, in the event of an emergency.

Tools

Keep a mini hammer, set of pliers, and an all-in-one screwdriver with interchangeable tips in a drawer in your kitchen. When a nut casing comes loose in the night, you won't have to rummage around in the garage for a simple screwdriver to fix it. The rest of your tools—larger hammers, channel lock wrenches, power tools, etc., should be stored in a proper toolbox that can be moved or wheeled to the job as necessary. (See the Resources section for woman-sized tools).

Toys

Teaching and enforcing good habits in children is a part of good parenting. They will pick up your habits, because that is what they know. You don't want their lives to be unmanageable, do you? Then teach them about the things they care a great deal about: Toys. Create at least three separate bins on the floor where they are easily accessed by very short people and won't topple over: one for soft toys, one for hard plastic toys, and one for books. Make a rule that kids must clean up at the end of every play period. (Time for dinner? Put away your toys first and then wash up.) When kids know where things go, they have an easier time taking care of their things. They also develop good organizational habits that will carry over into their adult lives. Kids should also learn where to put their dirty clothes each time they change.

A Junk Drawer

Every home should have a junk drawer. You have complete permission to create one—an unwieldy, unstructured catchall drawer for items that come into your house without a readily assigned official location. If your pack rat tendency is bigger than a junk drawer and you need a junk closet, then you must purchase stacking bins first and pile them up, so there is a semi-organized structure within your junk closet. Get a permanent marker and write on the bins: Batteries. Tools. Toys. Makeup. When you can't find something in the place it's supposed to be, there's always the junk drawer as a last resort.

Out of Sight, Out of Mind

When it comes to organization, the adage "out of sight, out of mind" can be either a blessing or a worry. After your first foray into organizing, those nice clean surfaces could be complicated by the burning question, "Where'd I put that?" Labeling is the answer. Buy a labeler, or use chalkboard paint to paint a small square on anything and write an erasable message in chalk. Chalkboard paint allows you to create instant chalkboard surfaces on walls, door insets, and containers—great not only for labels but for TO DO lists and GOAL lists as well. Keeping goal lists visible is a way to stimulate activity toward reaching them. Remember what we said about out of sight, out of mind? Not good for goals. Using blue painter's masking tape, square off an area that would make a handy message board and then paint the inset. It's terrific for children's rooms. Best of all, erasable labels allow containers to quickly change function as required.

The Organization Shower

Our culture has created ways to help newlyweds and expectant parents set up for the change about to happen in their life. But not everyone is going to be a bride or a mother. More people are choosing not to make that life choice. But they still need help from their friends and family to embark on independent living.

Enter the organization shower. Throwing a party for a friend or family member is a great way to discuss strategies, connect socially, and help out. Include great-looking storage items like boxes, bins, desk sets, message and schedule boards, hangers, shelving solutions, baskets, furniture, tools, pot hangers, key hooks, drawer dividers, chalkboard paint, labelers, and other organizers in your gift list. An organization shower is an excellent way to be there for someone who needs help creating a healing Emotional House.

HOUSE JOURNAL

Take a look at your HOTSPOTS. The areas that cause you the most stress or embarrassment, are the most congested or disorganized, and contain the most junk—all of these need reorganization. Make a list of them for your HOUSE PLAN and add in the number of bins, baskets, hooks, hangers, racks, laundry baskets, wardrobe valets, shoe trees, drawer separators, canisters, toolboxes, organizers, shelves, and labeling solutions you will need to accommodate each area.

⚜{ 15 }⚜

HOUSE RULE #7
Art Is Smart

*Install at least one objet d'art in every room in your house,
including the kitchen and the bathroom.*

If music is elevated speech, then art is elevated vision. It is an enhanced view of our experience in the world. Art bypasses cognitive thought and goes straight to the brain in a nonverbal way—connecting you with your spirit and expanding your vision past the confines of time and space. Anthropologists suggest ancient people thought art was magic … and maybe they were right. Art has the ability to transport you from the mundane to the transcendent in a heartbeat—from the hustle and bustle of an urban existence to the serenity of a pastoral English landscape, from the cut-and-dried realities of daily life to the colorful vision of an abstract expression that changes every time you look at it.

Art is important to every part of your being: your emotions, your mind, your spirit. It offers expression when there are no words and it offers a change in mood when there are no options. Think back over your life to the creative artworks you've seen in others' homes. What they displayed told you something about who they were. What we take in visually stays with us in a surprisingly unconscious way. This is why owning and displaying art in an Emotional House is "smart." Because you want to engage your being at all levels, even the subconscious.

Your Choice of Art Reflects on You

Probably nothing in your home says as much about you as the art you hang on your walls. It is the greatest indication of your depth, style, sensitivity, humor, and yes, even your intellect. But don't be intimidated: these things are intrinsic to who you are. Choosing art is nothing more than finding the images that speak to you—in a manner that you can receive every day.

Some libraries have art collections that allow you to check a painting out like a book and hang it in your home for a week or two. If yours doesn't have that option, visit galleries, museums, and crafts fairs when you can, and take note of the art displayed everywhere you go, including public places, restaurants, and friends' homes. Go beyond thinking "that will cover that wall" or "that doesn't clash with the sofa" or "that will impress my tragically hip friends." Instead, take your time and keep checking into your thoughts and feelings when you browse, seeking the feelings and thoughts you want to bring into your home. Choose what you like, what speaks to you, what stimulates reflection, rests your mind, and buoys your spirit, because it will frame your memories.

> DISPLAY ART AT EYE LEVEL FOR MAXIMUM IMPACT.

Family Photographs as Art

When we talk about art in this chapter, we are not talking about a spread of family photos on your walls. While we love family portraits as part of your memorabilia collection, art is in a very different category. Art can be paintings (oils, acrylics, or watercolors), pastels, charcoals, sculpture, pottery, line drawings, lithographs, silk screens, woven works, crafts, woodcuts, bronze busts, and more, but art is not a snapshot from your family's summer vacation. How is art, and yes, photographic art is included here, different from family photos? Each piece is impressionistic in nature. It is not necessarily the documentation of a moment in time. It is an artist's perspective on the subject. Without perspective, there is only a record—documentation, not art.

> USE ART TO CREATE A FOCAL POINT IN A FEATURELESS ROOM.

Even abstract art conveys a unique point of view of the world expressed through color and form. But understanding art isn't just about comprehending "what the artist intended," it's more about how you experience the vision yourself. And that's powerful. Art releases us from the repetition of habitual thought and allows us a fresh perspective. That's why it endures.

A Smile on Your Wall

A gallery owner in Paris's fashionable Place des Vosges Square relayed the story of a customer who made her first foray into the art world while vacationing there. This woman, who'd never purchased art before, bought a whimsically provocative painting by a fiery young Spanish artist for the price of $4,000. Shocked by her impulsive and uncharacteristic outlay of such a large sum, one that conclusively ended her holiday, she left in a whirlwind of panic, afraid about what she had done. The gallery owner grinned, explaining that the customer came back years later to report that it was the best money she'd ever spent. It topped any vacation by leaps and bounds. Her reason: "Every day, there is a smile on my wall."

Art should be a smile on your wall. And you can have it even on a budget. Local arts and craft fairs have wonderful bargains, and there are always flea markets and the attic of your old Aunt Hattie to rifle through for treasures. College exhibitions, galleries, and auctions are places you can find original art from new and emerging artists. There is nothing like owning original pieces, but if you can't afford this, there are always reproductions, prints, and posters of established works to thrill your eyes.

POSITION ART IN GROUPS TO MAKE PATTERNS

STRIPES—a vertical or horizontal line of art
PLAIDS—a square or a checkered layout
HERRINGBONE—an ascending slope up stairwells

Anchoring a Room with Art

Art anchors a room's theme. Whether it's a setting, a period style, a color, or a pattern motif you are going for, a dominant piece of art helps to define the space as a whole. Art is generally hung at eye level so it will be one of the first things you see when you enter a space. When a piece of artwork doesn't fit with the rest of the room, it is jarring, feels out of place, and disrupts the balance. You will feel strangely disturbed by the contrasting visuals.

A couple who have decorated their living room with stuffed animals, vintage children's toys, and comfortably casual furnishings have prominently hung a large painting with sexual themes that some might consider pornographic. The painting, one assumes, is meant to be amusing or, at least, thought-provoking, but the content sends a strident message that contradicts the rest of the room and puts everyone who enters off-balance. While the overall theme invites you to settle in, have fun, and engage your inner child, you can't help but feel the presence of this confrontational image looming over you, suggesting that it may not be safe to do so here.

Art can be used to provoke and disturb, as sociopolitical artists of the Dada movement in the early twentieth century and the feminist art movement of the '60s and '70s did. But you will more likely want to choose art pieces that contain complementary content to anchor your overall theme—unless throwing people off-balance is your mission in life. Keep in mind that this is the image you are choosing to greet you every day. The substance of your anchor has impact. If it's too much, it will sink your theme, and if it's too little, it will set your theme adrift. (See our website for a brief primer on some of the major art movements and tips on framing.)

The Art Under Your Feet

"A rug is a piece of art on your floor," says Rahmat Moradzdeh, owner of Pars Oriental Rug Gallery in Los Angeles. Look down. If there's no art there, you need new rugs. Floor coverings dominate a room's overall look, setting the tone. And tone always makes the music. Some of the more beautiful Persian rugs, like the silk Tabriz and Qums, are intricately woven masterpieces that will bring you endless joy and increase in value with age and wear.

Naturally, you must consider your lifestyle or the use of the room when choosing your floor art, but make the choice attractive and worthy. Floor coverings do have an impact on your psyche. You probably have the color, texture, and smell of that sculpted mustard green carpet from your childhood home or that filthy orange acrylic shag in your boyfriend's dorm room etched into your brain forever. So, you see their impression.

> ARRANGE THEMATIC PIECES OF ARTWORK TOGETHER TO TELL A STORY.

When purchasing an area rug for your home, buy the highest quality you can afford and, if at all possible, purchase organic products like wool, cotton, or silk-wool blends that aren't doused with chemicals and won't emit toxic gases that cause problems for respiratory systems. A beautiful piece of floor art will make every journey from A to B in your home a scenic route.

Art as a Healing Experience

A client, Louise, who refers to her childhood home as the House of Narcissism, realized there had not been a single stick of art anywhere in it. Instead, giant framed mirrors were hung prominently in every room—a detail that served the self-absorption of both her parents. This realization brought her to the understanding of why she had left all the walls in her home blank. But instead of shielding her from the painful memories of the past, the blank walls only served to call out to the absence of a nurturing parent.

In an attempt to reshape her unrelenting feeling of abandonment, Louise changed the atmosphere of her home by plastering it with inexpensive reproductions of the masterpieces she had seen on a field trip with an encouraging teacher whom she dearly loved. Art has that way of cutting to the heart of the matter. It's a healing tool that can affect mood and disposition. Perhaps that's why mental-health institutions use art therapy as a treatment.

The Artist Within

Everybody has an artist inside them: Your home is your canvas. You paint the picture of your past, present, and future life every day by how you organize your possessions, arrange your furniture, and live with your things. Allowing yourself to get creative, break out of old habits and find a way to express yourself not just *at* home but *with* your home, enlivens and enriches your daily experience. Think how a child feels when she comes home from kindergarten with her very first drawing and Mom takes the paper like it's a precious work of art and ceremoniously puts it up on the fridge for everybody to see: thrilled. That child is enlivened by her own creative need to express something personal and further enriched when Mom cherishes it, too.

In your home, you are both the child who expresses and the mom who cherishes. You paint the wall turquoise and antique it with gold; you stand back and ooh and ahh. You find the perfect vase at an art fair that brings out both the turquoise and the gold and place it at just the right angle to anchor the room. You find the antique frame that fits your handwoven sampler to a T and find the perfect place on the wall that pulls your room together. That's how an artist works: using familiar materials: seeing, finding, and imagining; and putting it all together. You've been doing it since you can remember. Trust it, risk new things (you can always change it back), and bring splash into your life. Try using the following exercise to inspire your own artist within:

Fashioning Your Anchor

1. Go to an art store and buy:

    *   A medium-sized canvas on a stretcher
    *   Five small jars of water-based paint that are colors you have in your home (from throw pillows, accessories, plants, etc.)
    *   A watercolor paintbrush, any size you want
    *   An artist's sponge

2. Go to a paint store (or your garage) and get:

    *   A quart of latex paint that is:

        a) the color of your wall (if your walls are colored), or

        b) the dominant color of your drapes, rug, or sofa (if your walls are white)

    *   A hot dog paint roller (the size of a hot dog and so-named)

3. Paint your canvas the color of your wall (or sofa, rug, or drape color) with the roller. Cover the canvas entirely. While the paint is still wet, take your small paintbrush and dip it in the most contrasting of the little jars that you bought and *splatter* it on the canvas. A little or a lot—it's up to you, you're the artist.

4. After it's dry, splatter, sponge, or roll (with a near-paintless roller) the other colors until you like the look. Vary this art project any way you'd like, bringing in other elements. Roll a swatch of fabric from your upholstery onto the canvas, painting it over. Glue photos or memorabilia onto the canvas. Stitch it with thread, or use a stamp or stencil to add letters or a pattern. Play! Leave some of the canvas blank. Sign it along the bottom in dark pencil. No need to frame it or anything—just hang it in a really good spot.

Congratulations! You have just engaged your inner artist and created an anchoring work of art for your own home. The theme is your room's color palette.

Check your HOTSPOTS for the room you designated as *least attractive*. You will want to add art elements to this space. Make a note in that room's section in your *Emotional House Design Binder*, and as you go about your business, seek out art pieces that might work well for that space. Put a smile on that wall.

HOUSE RULE #8
Set Boundaries for Room Use

*Set rules to clarify which activities and individuals are
permitted in each room—and stick to them!*

Your home is full of boundaries that divide one thing from another. The roof over your head, the floor beneath your feet, and the exterior walls that keep them apart set a boundary not only between indoors and outdoors, but between indoor and outdoor behavior—"Use your indoor voice!"

The divisions between rooms give you privacy and separate one kind of activity from another. There might also be boundaries within a room that divide one use of it from another—a shoji screen that divides a dining area from a conversation area in a New York loft; a kitchen counter that divides the cooking section from the family room in an open-concept apartment. But because boundaries involve making rules, many people have as hard a time setting them in rooms as they do setting them in relationships. Harmony and balance require parameters to be maintained, just as keeping your home life supportive and stress-free doesn't happen magically. Sometimes you have to insist. Boundaries are one of the most complicated issues for practical as well as emotional reasons. This chapter offers solutions.

We've found that people can be uncomfortable setting boundaries because they associate them with negative or painful experiences of rejection or punishment or powerlessness. But boundaries needn't feel alien or punitive; they are simply ways of defining what's appropriate in one area as opposed to another. And sometimes making a rule is the only way to do that.

Having boundaries actually brings a greater sense of security to all. It's reassuring to know the guidelines. You feel safer. If there were no traffic laws, imagine the road rage and treacherous driving conditions entering an intersection would present. Personal boundaries give definition and structure to living, too, making it easier and safer for all.

In order to ensure your rooms provide you with the basic needs they are built for and the emotional needs they are designed for, you need to set boundaries for their use. Sometimes you can make them flexible—like eating and doing homework at the kitchen table. And sometimes you need to set rules—"no napping in the dryer"—to protect spaces meant for specific purposes as well as those who use them.

Setting Boundaries

Some spaces are naturally problem areas and they all involve private space: these are the bedrooms, the home office, and your workshop or studio space. Most people give themselves permission to take space for work, because while we may not respect the need to be alone, be creative, or even be intimate as we should, we do respect the need to make money. Nevertheless, if you work at home, you have doubtless encountered difficulty defining work space and work time. Making a rule and holding everyone to it can help.

For example: "I work from 9 A.M. to 3 P.M., and from 9 P.M. to 11 P.M. in my office in the garage and am not to be disturbed" is a reasonable boundary to set if you work or run a small business from your home and your family's very security is dependent on that income.

Holding to that rule is as much a matter of respecting your own boundaries as it is one of demanding self-discipline. It is no different if the boundary is around private time to think, to be alone with your significant other, to develop a new business, or to read, watch a game, create artwork, tinker mechanically, sew, garden, or anything. Difficulty in defining boundaries for time and space usage appears to be a practical concern, but it is really an *emotional* issue.

Difficulties Setting Boundaries

Those who have difficulties holding and even defining boundaries usually feel like they don't deserve them. They have elevated others' needs above their own. Women and men both find it hard to hold space separate from spouses. Parents often have trouble when it comes to kids. Even younger children need help setting boundaries with their older siblings. In every case, however, it is well worth the effort to learn how. Because boundaries are at the heart of the support cornerstone.

Children and Boundaries

Dr. Phil McGraw, author of the popular *Life Strategies* books, has said that when his children were little, he told them something to the effect that, "When Mommy and Daddy's bedroom door is closed, you can't come in, period. And unless someone is bleeding to death or the house is on fire, you better not even knock." His point is a good one: You deserve sanctuary in your home even if you have children, so you have to put limits on your children's behavior to protect it.

A participant in a Spiritual Housecleaning workshop protested that she had no sanctuary in her house because her son's toys were in her bedroom. Why? "Because it has a good carpet." Okay, if her child were two years old, it might be easier to have him here than to be in his room with him. But the boy was seven, and she didn't want to restrict his freedom to play where he wanted. "Besides, he likes to have toys in every room, just in case . . ."

Moms and Dads out there, if you don't teach your kids that their rights are limited when it comes to your or anyone's personal space, property, or rights, then you are creating little bullies. Anyone who exerts the power of "Yes I can" without the limits of "I really shouldn't" is a tyrant, no matter what age they are. Little bullies grow up to be bigger problems; teach them now.

Learning responsibilities like respect for other people's rights should start as soon as children can understand what no means. Begin teaching them the right to say no and the responsibility to respect no by setting rules for certain rooms: Don't jump on the couch in the living room; do knock on the bathroom door if it's closed; don't knock on the bedroom door unless you're on fire; don't play in Mommy's office *ever*. If your kids need quality time with you, a place to jump, a place to play, make time and space for those things; but don't sacrifice the spaces that provide for your emotional (or financial) needs to do it. Having your needs met makes it easier to meet theirs. That way everyone gets support.

In your HOUSE JOURNAL, name three boundaries you need to set in your home to get the support you need. Then, jot these future boundaries down in the corresponding ROOM section in your *Emotional House Design Binder*. When you start working on that room in Part III, you'll have an action to take, which will move your home closer to Emotional House status.

Enforcing Boundaries

Children need boundaries as much as parents need them. That includes childproofing barriers (visit our website, www.emotionalhouse.com, for a good list). But it's when children don't know what the rules are that they are likely to feel unsafe and start testing them and acting out. Then you don't get your space and your kids don't feel safe.

A father of two who worked at home started finding it difficult to find quiet time as his daughter became a toddler. He and his wife decided to refit the garage into a freestanding home office to save money on an off-site office. He retrofitted the garage and looked forward to having the privacy to focus, without his toddler's noise interrupting him at crucial moments. But it never happened that way. He neglected to claim his office or make it a child-free space. In fact, it became the best playroom in the house. In no time, all the three-year-old's blankies and stuffies collected there amongst the seven-year-old's balls and trucks. It was the place the older one ran to as soon as he came home from school. Daddy's office had become a very expensive, though ill-equipped, nursery. Now he was still in the position of stealing time and space for himself and it was he who suffered.

Asked why he didn't keep the kids out, he said he didn't want them to go through the rejection he'd experienced when locked out of his father's study. But in fact, he was being locked out from his work and reenacting his childhood experience himself.

Boundaries are necessary to keep activities separate. Playing with your kids is important, but there's a time and there's a place—and it's not all the time and it's not every space. You not only have a right to keep them out of your private spaces when you need to work or to have alone time, you have a responsibility to yourself as well as to them to teach them how to understand and respect these boundaries.

Make boundaries for yourself, your housemates, or your houseguests for that matter, especially when self-discipline or emotional upheaval is a problem in your world. One of the authors who found herself newly single made a boundary that she would not eat dinner alone in front of the TV—a depressing experience for her. Instead, each evening she set a beautiful table in the dining area with candles, wine, and music for company, and rebonded with her *inner* beloved. Personal boundaries can pave the road to healing in an Emotional House. Whether it's "don't traipse mud across the carpet" or "don't hang your underwear on the doorknob," these boundaries don't restrict freedoms as much as they define parameters and respect needs. If you need workshop space or a playroom or a mudroom or a place to put dirty clothes, make a space for it; but don't ruin the function of another room or violate the rights of another person to do it.

Do your best to communicate boundaries in a positive manner to the members of your household. Explain that you need these boundaries and will be an easier person to live with if they are respected. Welcome a discussion about the boundaries those who are present would also like to have respected. It opens the lines of communications to meet everyone's needs, instead of making others feel attacked.

Divide and Conquer

In House Rule #1: Live In Your Whole House (chapter 9), you were instructed to make note in your HOUSE PLAN of the emotional and practical functions that were missing from the current setup of your home. Get out that list now. Pick one function that your home doesn't serve from that list and follow along.

Making Rooms Multifunctional

By physically setting boundaries and creating dual-purpose rooms, you can add these functions to your home, remove chaos, and add balance to your living situation. How do you do this? Simple. Define task-oriented spaces and install physical boundaries (like dividers) to separate them.

A living room can be both a meeting area and a bill-keeping area, or have a conversation pit, a reading corner, and a tidy breakfast spot; and it all can be achieved by strategic placement of furniture and accessories. Even small spaces can be multipurposed if you take the time to think about assigning appropriate and complementary tasks to the space.

Consider the Blending of Tasks

Start by honoring the room's main function before deciding which tasks to combine. A missing dining area can easily be added to a living room, for instance. Both spaces have complementary functions: bonding and camaraderie. But you don't want to put your sewing table in the kids' playroom, where little feet could encounter the danger of pins and needles. Similarly, a study in the main living room is not an ideal location if you need to concentrate while the other occupants of the household gather for raucous video game competitions. But many tasks are harmoniously paired and can actually enhance the functionality of the whole house by creating the effect of having additional rooms. Isn't this true with relationships as well? A friend from school more easily becomes your accountant than your neighbor becomes your proctologist. It's all in the situation. So the first law of multifunctioning is to consider the blend of tasks the room will be servicing.

Review the list of missing emotional and practical functions you noted in your HOUSE PLAN and pick rooms where you can blend in these functions. For example:

ROOM	TASK 1	TASK 2
Kitchen	Food prep & dining	Bill-keeping nook

Determine Your Equipment and Furnishing Needs

After you decide which areas will marry well, make a list of the furnishings and accessories you think may be required for the new functions. Walk yourself through the task mentally—what do you need? If you are creating a bill-paying area in your kitchen, you'll need a desktop, chair, good task lighting (remember the comfort factor), a filing system or filing box for records, and a storage area for newly arriving unpaid bills to gather. You'll also need good organizational concepts for regular usage items, a bulletin board to post your financial plan, and an inspiration element like a goal board or art object to enliven that area.

Make certain you also know the location of your existing power outlets. AC power outlets will be a determining factor for the location of items that require power, like task lighting, unless you want to live with a tangle of cords running across the floor that could cause accidents in high-traffic areas.

Put your list in the appropriate ROOM section in your *Emotional House Design Binder* where the new function will reside—in this case, the KITCHEN section. And refine your list as you move further through the House Rules and decide there are other things you want to add. You'll reassess your shopping lists later in chapter 21, A Journey through Your Home, when you prioritize by budget.

Now that you have your list of furniture and equipment, the next step is to create a floor plan for the whole room, incorporating all tasks.

Measure and Prep

In order to prepare for your new layouts, you need to assess your existing space and furnishings. Measuring the room's area and the furniture inside it allows you to make cutout templates of furniture and your floor area to experiment with on graph paper. Preparing floor plan mock-ups (like designers do) is the best way to find creative solutions when multifunctioning, and it's a lot easier than the backbreaking task of moving furniture. If you want to start now, there are detailed instructions on how to measure and create your mock-ups in chapter 21. Or you can wait until you begin the actual work on each room.

Group and Arrange the Furniture for Each Task

After furniture and room templates are made, the next step is to experiment with room layouts. Remember, the main function of the room should take up the most real estate, but the secondary function you are adding doesn't have to be shoved into a corner. What you're trying to create are demarcation boundaries. For example, if you are multifunctioning a living room and dining area, each area can easily be defined with an area rug or table that anchors the task area. The furniture is arranged around it. But you can undertake more creative solutions.

INSTANT ROOM DIVIDERS

Rummage through garage sales for empty picture frames. Paint them to match your room's dominant wall color and suspend them from the ceiling with similarly-colored braided rope to create the illusion of a floating wall.

Think about how your favorite restaurants have arranged their spaces. Designers of eating establishments are masters at creating multifunctional rooms. Inside one large space they'll often have waiter's stations, buffet services, dessert stands, bars, coat checks, a cashier, reception area, and of course, the individual dining areas or booths. Yet each section seems to be a completely separate area. Restaurants use implied dividers—a bank of planters, water feature, piece of sculpture, etched glass, even hanging art and sheer draperies. You can do all this, too.

An inexpensive but great trick to divide a living area is to create the illusion of a wall. In the living room for instance, by situating your sofa in the middle of the room on an area rug, instead of cramming it up against a wall, you can place a sofa table behind it and hang an empty picture frame from the ceiling at eye level above the sofa table (out of harm's way). Suspend the frame with fishing wire or a braided silk rope, depending on the look you want, or hang it in front of a sheer drapery. Placing tall potted plants, sculptures, or floor lamps behind the sofa also helps create the impression of a wall where there isn't one, while not closing in the room. In the case of the empty frame, your eye is allowed to see through to the other task area, but registers the frame as a demarcation point at the same time. You can also use bookshelves, a group of candle stands, plants, or even an interior water feature, which masks sound, to divide a room. Try hanging a drapery rod partially across the ceiling and draping half of a swag curtain across part of the room to create a demarcation point. Try to think outside the box. We have even seen small halfwalls constructed out of drywall and framing that completely

section off on area while not extending to the ceiling. These marvelous floating barriers (which can be moved like a stage set) allow for artwork to be mounted and provide an extra spot for a sideboard or cabinet.

Decide which technique most appeals to you to demarcate the tasks in your multifunctional rooms. Make a note of these in the appropriate ROOM sections of your *Emotional House Design Binder*. Add any items needed to achieve this to your shopping list.

Create a Focal Point for Each Task Area

Creating a focal point for each task area is another excellent way to help with demarcation. Focal points can easily be achieved with rugs, art, color, bold fabrics, or special architectural or accessory features like a fireplace, art piece, built-ins, aquarium, picture windows, and especially lighting. The focal point is the item your eye is drawn to and around which the task of the area revolves. It gives definition to the location, so make sure your focal point sets the mood and theme you want for that task. You don't want your eye settling on that unwieldy pile of unpaid bills on the floor, when it could be drawn to the unique tiffany shade hovering above your polished rolltop desk. Every task area should have a focal point that defines the area and the mood of the space. Make it a positive one.

Decide on focal points for each of the task areas in your multifunctional room. Write these down in the designated ROOM section in your *Emotional House Design Binder*. For example:

	TASK 1: LIVING ROOM	TASK 2: DINING AREA
Focal Point	Fireplace mantel	Table centerpiece

Tie the Theme of the Room Together

Finally, tie the multifunctioned room together with color, pattern, texture, theme, or furniture style. Coordinating the overall look gives a sense of uniformity to the room. Whatever your budget or style choice, make sure that the area functions practically and emotionally and incorporates well into the main design style of the greater room. Adding a bold splash of color in the secondary area that matches the dominant color of the main area's focal point is also a great trick of the trade. Perhaps it's a pretty box to hold the bills as they arrive on your desk or a vase of silk flowers that match the sofa at the other end of the room—whatever the item, let it tie the look together.

In the ROOM sections in your *Emotional House Design Binder*, write down your ideas for the theme (color, pattern, texture, setting, style) that you will carry through each space.

You now have all the steps, so let's recap.

Recap—To Multifunction a Room

- Consider the blending of tasks first.

- Make a list of furnishings, equipment, and accessories for each task.

- Measure and prepare a floor plan with scaled-down cutouts of furniture.

- Arrange the furniture for each area on paper first, allowing for traffic flow.

- Anchor each area with a rug or other demarcation boundary.

- Divide the sections with strategically placed furniture, shelves, or accessories.

- Create a focal point for each section.

- Tie the room's look together with theme, color, or style.

Safety and Security—The Ultimate Boundary

Now let's talk about the most important boundary of all—the safety and security of your home, both from outside intruders and from inside dangers. Safety and security can be enhanced by strengthening your home's perimeters as well as your personal parameters.

First and foremost, your home *must* be free of physical and emotional abuse and must not nurture illicit activities that endanger you or your property. An atmosphere of constant fear about what "might happen" neither feeds the spirit nor makes for a happy life. Remove any individual from the home or your personal hemisphere who brings this emotional roller coaster into your life. If you are unable to remove them, remove yourself and get safe. If you have children who are in danger, remove them. If it's a child bringing the danger to your home, seek professional help immediately. You can't create an Emotional House under these conditions.

In terms of outside dangers, that is something you cannot control completely. No home is impervious to the determined intruder, but there are measures you can take to reduce the likelihood that your residence will become a target. Start by reviewing your baseline security condition (the one you identified in the Residence Logistics section in chapter

4) and make a list of the places you feel vulnerable, both inside your home and in exterior locations like your entryway, yard, exterior storage, or garage:

_____   _____   _____

_____   _____   _____

A roll of duct tape won't secure your home, but there are other surprisingly inexpensive measures you can take to shore up its security. Your first line of defense is your door. Install deadbolt locks on all doors and window stops (in addition to the sash lock) on every window in your home. Trim bushes and brush around the home to eliminate fire hazards and hiding spots for potential intruders. Install security lighting inside and out.

Exterior floods with movement sensors, which burst on when someone moves past, are excellent deterrents. Security lights with photoelectric cells, which switch on at dusk and off at dawn, are an energy-efficient alternative. Add an alarm system as perimeter security whether you live in an apartment or a house. Battery-operated versions that stick onto windows and doors are available for mere dollars; hardwired versions can be contracted with a security company. Programmable timers on your interior lights are another good option.

Home protection is one thing that should not be taken lightly. Whether you own or rent, set strong boundaries and keep your place safe. If your home doesn't already have each of these safety and security items, put them on your shopping list in your HOUSE PLAN today:

- Deadbolts for all doors

- Window locks and window stops

    - Smoke and carbon monoxide detectors

        - Fire extinguisher

            - Alarm system (battery operated at minimum)

            - Exterior and interior security lighting

            For a more extensive explanation of other security options, visit our website.

❧{ 17 }❧

HOUSE RULE #9
If It's Broke, Fix It

Get a tool kit and minor repair supplies and build your Reliable Referrals list.

Your home is a living, breathing entity that requires unflinching care. It has a skeletal system and it has skin. If you concentrate on décor but ignore the bones, in no time you'll have water damage, dry rot, an unsound roof, a crumbling foundation, and more. Ignore the skin and your paint will chip, wallpaper will fade, dust mites will proliferate, and stale unhealthful air will fill your home. Clothing a sick body in fancy outfits will only disguise the problem and leave the essential being uncared for. In other words, upkeep and repair trump decorating when a choice must be made.

When things start to break in your home, your Emotional House becomes stressful. It's the simple things that get you, like a burned-out bulb when you want to read, a dripping faucet that runs up your water bill just when you're facing a budget crunch, or a roaring refrigerator motor that makes your kitchen sound more like NASCAR than nurturance.

If repairs are neglected, they will impede the use of your house, destroy your chances of creating a stress-free environment, and undermine the physical support your home is designed to give you, one broken room at a time. That's the reason for this rule.

TOOL TIP

Always keep a small tool set and faucet washers in a kitchen drawer so you can fix leaks and easy repairs immediately. Call in professionals for major plumbing, electrical work, and structural preservation.

A Stitch in Time Saves Nine

Everything needs repair eventually, and the longer you wait to fix something, the more it will cost you. Paying attention to minor repairs can prevent major damage. If you own your home, it's vital to assemble a list of reliable repair personnel before problems happen. Ask neighbors for referrals. They will be more than willing to share the names of service workers they like and the ones to stay away from. If you rent and are at the mercy of a difficult landlord, you have two choices—find better lodging or incur the costs of doing minor repairs yourself. The relief factor is always worth the effort *and* the few extra bucks—consider it the price of taking care of yourself.

Whatever your situation, you should acquire how-to repair manuals and a good repair and tool kit that is well stocked (ask for tool kits as gifts at birthdays and holidays).

How-To Books That Should Be in Your Library

- A complete guide to home plumbing

- A complete guide to home wiring

- A complete guide to home repair

How-to books on home repairs not only inform you how to fix things, they also inform you of the basics of the job: the materials and tools required and the approximate amount of time and labor required by someone who knows what they're doing. You need this information *before* you hire someone to do it. Black & Decker, Better Homes & Gardens, Home Depot, and Lowe's all put out some terrific how-to books that take you right through from beginning to end of anything that you might encounter, with colorful pictures. And Lowe's has a marvelous DIY website full of great tips.

Always read up on the repair before you hire a professional. Speak the lingo so contractors will know that they can neither do a shoddy job nor rip you off. And with that respect comes better workmanship. For smaller repairs, keep some simple tools handy.

Your Repair Kit

PLUMBING KIT

- Assortment of washers
- Plumber's tape
- Silicone sealer
- Caulk
- Plunger
- Toilet snake

ELECTRICAL KIT

- Extra light bulbs for all your fixtures (in the correct wattages)
- Extra fuses (in the correct amperages)
- Fuse puller
- Wire cutter and stripper
- Black electrical tape
- Rubber-insulated needle-nose pliers
- Assorted wire end-caps
- Circuit tester

CARPENTRY AND BASIC TOOL KIT

- Hammer
- Regular pliers and needle-nose pliers
- Adjustable wrench
- Channel lock wrench (ladies, this baby is leverage where you don't have strength)
- A set of C-wrenches or a ratchet set (metric and U.S. sizes)
- Screwdrivers (flat, Phillips, and hexagonal/Allen wrench)
- Saws: wood saw, hacksaw (optional power models are jigsaw and circular saw)
- Cordless power drill
- Assortment of nails, screws, and picture hangers

Three Things Everyone Needs to Know—
Renters and Home Owners Alike

1. How to turn off the water to your home and each faucet

2. Where your fuse box or circuit breaker box is (and how to replace fuses)

3. How to turn off the gas

Never make any repairs to plumbing or electric without turning off the water or power, respectively. Leave gas line repairs to professionals.

Hiring a Contractor—Referrals and References

After you have informed yourself as to *how* to fix whatever's "broke" and sought out a professional, check their references and contact your state's license board to ensure that their licenses and insurance bonds are current and valid. State licensing boards keep records of the lawsuits and complaints against contractors. Some unscrupulous contractors use phony or suspended licenses and some even their driver's licenses to get jobs, so it's important to check. Also review their portfolios or go see other jobs that they've done. Don't hire if you don't feel comfortable. Call someone else.

Finally, always get contractors and their subcontractors to sign a liability release form in case they are hurt on the job (these are available at most office supply stores) and have their *sub*contractors sign waiver and release forms when you make your final payment. If the contractor is paid in full, but doesn't pay the subcontractors, they can come after you for payment. They have the legal right to place a mechanical lien on your home, which prevents you from selling it when you're ready, until they are paid. Seems unfair, but it's the law in some states, so get those forms signed at time of final payment.

A NOTE ABOUT CONTRACTORS' JOB ESTIMATES

Expect time and cost overruns. Whatever the job estimate, double it.

The Emotional Stress of Major Repairs

Having construction done in your home or apartment is an extremely stressful event. The whole *balance* of your *support* structure is off, and you will find yourself starting to get irritable. Before any major repair, sit down with your family and prepare them for this inevitability. Explain that while tempers will flare, everyone is still loved and cherished. It is more than just the emotional stress that the physical disruption brings, it is also the degree of toxicity from gypsum and floating plaster dust and such in the air that can play havoc with the human immune system and emotions. If at all possible, try to remind yourself and your coinhabitants in advance that during one of the temper flare-ups (and there will be some), if anyone has a clear head, they must become the "designated level-head" who reminds everyone that it's the construction toxicity talking, not the person. It is extremely important to get out of a residence that is being overhauled and spend some time in saner environments with working systems and fresh air. It will do everyone a world of good.

Cleanup After a Major Repair

When the job is done, be sure to factor in at least three days of cleanup. Budget in a cleaning service to give you some relief. Walls will need to be washed, vents will need to be vacuumed, and upholstery and draperies will often need dry-cleaning. Even if you covered your belongings with plastic sheeting, which is recommended, some degree of dust will penetrate, so factor in the extra time.

Now review the rooms on your HOTSPOT list that you nominated as needing repair. Note each of them in the ROOM sections of your *Emotional House Design Binder*. If the repair is one you can handle, add the how-to book you need to your Shopping List. After you review the advice in the how-to book, add all the repair items you will need to your Shopping List as well. If you require a contractor, begin asking neighbors for recommendations. Create a RELIABLE REFERRALS & CONTACTS section in your *Emotional House Design Binder* and add the names to it. Put the job on your TO DO list and get it done before you mess around with décor. Remember, repair trumps decorating when a choice must be made.

HOUSE RULE #10
The Divine Is in the Details

Establish a minimum of two divine details in each room.

I t's not the engine of your home, but it sure is the switch that turns the engine on. It's the thing you notice when you're searching for an apartment or home—that extra special feature like a carved mantel, crown moldings, built-in wall niches, beautiful tile in the kitchen, arched doorways, wainscoting, a garden fountain, and more. Divine details just make you feel better about your home, and that's nothing to sneeze at. You don't have to be rich to experience those extra details. If your home or apartment doesn't already have these structural gifts, adornments can be added even on a meager budget, and you might be surprised when you can suddenly hear that engine purr. That's what harmony sounds like. And isn't it just *divine, dahling?*

Divine details don't have to be nailed down or glued to the wall to make a difference. Little extras like a table runner topped with a centerpiece, a backlit vase of fresh flowers, a painted birdcage filled with dangling ivy, or just changing out outdated knobs on your cabinet doors can pick up the ambience of a room in a heartbeat. Throws—whether blankets, pillows, or cushions—in bold fabrics are instant divine detail elements, and they come in a variety of shapes and sizes, good for cozying up and for utilization as lumbar, knee, or neck supports.

Decorative ironwork is divine when combined with foliage, while a painted window box with herbs on your kitchen windowsill serves two masters—the presence of a divine detail and the enjoyment of interior gardening providing a harvest of gastronomic delight. If you have a dangling light cord in a closet, clip on a decorative pull (even your closets can delight you). Add a scalloped edge of fringe to bland blinds or silk tassels to swagged curtains. Begin instilling your private refuge with divine details today and just watch the homey atmosphere blossom.

It's All in the Bevel—Mirrors

Mirrors are an easy place to start adding divine elements to your home's décor. They are a secret weapon of designers and, when placed strategically on one wall, trick the eye into giving the impression of a larger space. Bookending a window with mirrors will bounce more light into a dark space. And putting one opposite a window will reflect the light and cast a wonderful glow everywhere.

A bevel in a mirror is a slanted depression in the surface of the glass around the edges. It adds a rich elegance to the surface—a very divine detail. Bevels increase the cost of a mirror just slightly, but they're still surprisingly affordable. Framed mirrors are a new trend in bathroom design and make great focal points as well. Replacing that boring medicine cabinet mirror with a framed, beveled, or etched mirror can really kick your divine factor up a level.

The Divine Naturals: Fire, Water, Light

Fireplaces

A fireplace is probably one of the most desired details in a home or apartment. The love of a flickering, crackling fire lies deep in our DNA—it means survival and brings unfathomable comfort. But if your dwelling wasn't so blessed, you don't have to embark on a major construction job to enjoy one. Even if you are a renter, you can purchase or create a faux fireplace that adds warmth to your surroundings. There are several options in addition to the traditional wood-burning fireplace or gas-powered firebox, both of which require chimneys.

Electric Fireplaces

Plug it in and enjoy. Electric fireplaces are starting to look more authentic. Internal fans blow heated air to warm the room and bring the illusion of a glimmering flame that sizzles almost like the real thing. The landlord can't fault you for this one.

RealFlame Fireplaces

If an electric fireplace doesn't do it for you, there's the RealFlame fireplace that burns smoke-free canned fuel gel and doesn't require venting. The gel is composed primarily of isopropyl alcohol and thickeners, according to resellers, and is considered pollution free by the Environmental Protection Agency. For the price of a club chair ($400–500) you can own a RealFlame fireplace that literally produces a real flame and is portable enough to move from room to room.

The Faux Fireplace

If you're budget conscious, you can hit yard sales and junk shops for a used fireplace surround or just build your own faux fireplace with a few pieces of molding and tile. Secure it to the wall with construction adhesive or hang it using heavy-duty picture hangers. Set a spray of candles in front (securely away from combustible wood) and you have an instant focal point and divine detail. Some apartment dwellers are creating these and hanging them just for the holidays to dangle their Christmas stockings over.

HOW TO DO IT

Go to the molding section of your home improvement store and buy:

- Two pilasters (the vertical side columns)
- A piece of wood to connect the columns horizontally
- Edge molding to top it
- Screws and fasteners
- Paint
- Heavy-duty picture hangers or construction glue to attach your mantel to the wall

Create your hearth floor with:

- A piece of WonderBoard (also known as backerboard)
- Ceramic or faux brick tiles
- A small container of premixed Thinset mortar mix

Lay down a smear of premixed Thinset on the WonderBoard. Press on your tiles and add a little mortar between them. Instant hearth. You can do the same for the back of your faux firebox. But remember there is no chimney, so place your candle fire on the tile hearth floor, well away from the wood. If you want a look with more of the depth of a natural firebox, build small boxed-out pilasters and hammer them onto WonderBoard for tiling. This sort of faux fireplace will be too heavy to hang on the wall and will have to be freestanding.

It's all easier to do than you can imagine, and everything is available at your home improvement store. Once you make one, you'll be experimenting with color, scrolled wood, and architectural adornments, and placing faux fireplaces in every room of your apartment or home.

Water Features

The lucky few who are blessed with ocean and lakefront properties know the value of mood enhancement that burbling water gives off. More and more medical studies are looking into the mental health effects of negative ions, but all you have to do is go to the beach to experience the stress relief and reconnection to the bigger picture that a body of water can bring. So introducing the divine element of running water into your home is a worthy effort.

The Indoor Tabletop Fountain

These are available everywhere today, at kitchen and bath stores, drugstores, and more, for under $20. But you can make your own for as little as $6 with nothing more than a bowl, a few river stones, and a bubbler pump from a hardware, hobby, garden, or online store. Instant tranquility. Feel the stress lifting? See our website for directions.

Larger-Scaled Fountains

Found at nurseries, these wonderful items offer cascading waterfalls flowing over etched glass, corrugated steel, and rocks. But they are more than fountains. They are excellent sound barriers as well as natural water sculptures (remember, Art Is Smart). Consider installing a large indoor fountain in areas where you need sound masking. (A smaller tabletop fountain in your guest powder room will serve two masters—a divine detail and a sound masker that will make your guests more comfortable in their privacy.)

The Magic of Light

Lighting is one of the most underestimated of design elements, yet it is probably *the* most important. Several table lamps scattered throughout will turn an austere room into a cozy hideaway. A small group of flickering candles will instantly create a romantic mood to remind the libido of its raison d'être, while 100 watts of light spilling across a comfy tub chair is an invitation to an evening with a good book. Directional shelf lighting can turn a dreary bookshelf into an art gallery, and splashes of small spotlights in the garden can theatrically mark a pathway to a secret garden. Always add an assortment of lighting choices to your living room to provide diverse atmospheres for different activities.

> Lighting all four corners of a room will make the space seem larger.

Lighting For Health

Studies show that installing light dimmers and dimming the light intensity near bedtime can help insomniacs' biorhythms sync up with nature's by informing their body clocks that it's time to close out the day. Full-spectrum lighting assists in defeating seasonal affective disorder (SAD), also known as the winter blues. Even if you don't have sleep problems or SAD, it's a good idea to bring natural light into your home and especially to any teenager's room that's been painted black.

Verilux is one maker of natural-spectrum lightbulbs, which they label as "Sunshine in a Box"—the purplish-hued bulbs are more expensive, but give off a unique glow. Halogen bulbs, which also resemble daylight, are useful but should always be used with caution because they burn at very high temperatures. Never place halogen light fixtures (like torchieres) near curtains or where they can be toppled. And *turn them off* when you leave the room!

> A low-hanging pendant light will define a focal point, like a breakfast table.

The Lighting Plan

Always design your lighting around the task at hand. A dark, moody bathroom is no good if it's the only place to apply makeup or shave, and klieg lights in the bedroom won't get you in the mood for much of anything. When creating a lighting plan for your rooms, first determine the task each will serve, then use the following three steps for the lighting design.

STEP ONE—AMBIENT LIGHTING

This is the overall room lighting, designed to wash the whole area. Good sources are ceiling lights, skylights, recessed lights that cast a downward glow, and torchieres that illuminate upward across the ceiling and then bounce light down. Use mirrors and white space to bounce and amplify light in dark areas.

STEP TWO—ACCENT LIGHTING

Supplement the overall lighting with accents such as table lamps, sconces, track lighting, directional eyeballs, valance lighting, and low-wattage lighting for artwork. A 40-watt incandescent bulb behind a Japanese rice paper shoji screen can light up a whole corner with little energy use. Providing ambient light *without* accent lighting is a no-no (and vice versa). The secret to a good lighting plan is all in the accents, which add instant dimension to your home—a divine detail.

STEP THREE—TASK LIGHTING

Finally, ensure you have good task lighting that is bright and clear. A 100-watt incandescent bulb, with the light cast downward and shining directly over the work area, is excellent for a desk or worktable. Under-cabinet lighting is a great plus in the kitchen and can be the difference between a workable prep area and a sliced finger. Purchase light fixtures that allow for movement and redirection. This is especially helpful for your computer area, where lamps require adjustment due to the glare that can reflect back from a monitor.

Taking the extra time to create a good lighting plan can be the difference between dullsville and divine elegance. And you do deserve a warm and inviting home, don't you?

HALOGEN BULBS

Avoid touching the bulb when changing lamps. The oil from fingers can cause bulbs to burn out prematurely.

Architectural Details

Everything you see in your home should elevate your living experience. But without trim, a cabinet is just a square box, and it's the same for the walls, doors, and windows of a home without molding. When someone says "that's a house with character," they are usually talking about architectural details like trim.

Molding Your Daily Experience with Architectural Details

Don't be afraid of molding suppliers. You don't have to be a contractor to shop, and you can buy anything from strips of chair-rail molding to carved finials, decorative rosettes, corbels, and scrolls—some for just a dollar or two. Apply them with a little construction glue or finishing nails and suddenly your flat walls and plain fireplace mantel pop. Renters can add architectural details too, with items like wooden or plaster medallions (usually available in Celtic or floral motifs), which can be painted or antiqued and hung on the wall or ceiling. Nonfunctional wooden shutters, hung with picture hangers for easy removal, can flank an inside window for an Old World look. Decorative scroll-carved corbels under a load-bearing shelf are divine replacements for cheap-looking metal casings and can transform the entire look of a shelving unit and create the illusion of a permanent architectural detail.

For homeowners, who have freedom to make more permanent changes, plate rails running along wall tops are wonderful places to display your treasures (secure these items in quake areas). And rosettes (tiny medallions used at the corners of woodwork, such as on door frames) really bring an elite look to a room. Friezes can easily be added now through plaster effects or with wallpaper (the Lincrusta wallpaper you were introduced to in chapter 7, Possessing Personal Style). Finally, crown molding around the edges of the ceiling is an addition you'll never regret, even if you struggle with mitered cuts and the difficult installation as a do-it-yourselfer. Installer's amnesia will soon be your friend as you enjoy the rich new detail you've added to your home.

Trompe l'Oeil—For a Room with a View

Finally, if you live in either a high-rise or basement apartment and always wished you could have a different view, you still can with a trompe l'oeil painting effect. Trompe l'oeil (a French term that means "to trick the eye") is a realistic style of three-dimensional painting designed to create the illusion that what's painted is *real*—like a stunning view out a painted window, or the ever popular recessed wall niche with vase. Artists who specialize in trompe l'oeil are expensive, but you can buy pre-made wallpaper, laminates on wood, and lithographs for virtually any budget.

Adding Your Divine Details

1. Review your HOTSPOTS list for the rooms designated as most embarrassing and unattractive. Form a new lighting plan for these rooms using the Three-Step Lighting Plan explained in this chapter. Put it on your TO DO list and add any lighting accessories you need to your shopping list in the pertinent ROOM section of your *Emotional House Design Binder*.

2. Determine new focal points for each of these rooms using another divine detail: a table centerpiece, a framed beveled mirror you hope to find at a yard sale, or something grander. Add it to your TO DO list and shopping list in the pertinent ROOM section of your *Design Binder*.

❧{ 19 }❧

HOUSE RULE #11
All White Is Not Right

Add some color to at least one wall in every room in your house.

That elusive pot of gold isn't found at the base of a white beam of light; it's only to be found at the end of a full-spectrum rainbow. That's because we need the diversity of color in our experience to receive all the golden riches life has to offer—color in design, color in art, color in people, relationships, encounters, and yes, even in jokes, though sometimes that's called "off-color" by the beige brigade. We are a multicolored people on a blue spinning planet with a vast array of needs, values, emotions, and beliefs. And within all that, there is color—hot and cold, bold and muted, shocking and neutral. Beautiful, undeniable color: a gift from the heavens, which we are meant to receive, and that is why all white is not right.

Color as a Personal Limiter

An all-white color scheme can become a lifestyle limiter, especially in carpeting. "Don't walk on the carpet!" is a statement that should *never* be heard in your home unless it's spoken to someone coming in with mud on their shoes. Carpets are floor coverings. Floors are meant to be trod upon. Make them a color receptive to that activity. Anytime a color scheme becomes a restrictive element in your home, you need to change it.

An associate, whom we'll call Anna, had an all-white house. Her walls, sofa, chairs, throw blankets, drapes, and area rugs were all white. It gave her a sense of purity and accentuated the control she had taken over her life, which had begun as the middle child in a family of violence and chaos where everything with her name on it either got wrecked by selfish siblings or taken away. Her only childhood solace was found in a small menagerie of pets she adored. Now, in her adult home, Anna wanted control over her environment. If her friends felt too nervous to relax in her living room, afraid of spilling something or leaving behind evidence of their visit, she didn't care: she liked the wholesome feeling all this white gave her, even if it now controlled her friends' behavior. Finally, her white world was serene and clean.

Then she fell in love with a man who brought over his dog, a spirited Jack Russell terrier, whom she loved equally well, and who was accustomed to being welcomed on furniture. And suddenly white was a most impractical design choice. The two things she realized had been missing in her life—love and animals—trumped control so completely that she started changing her décor to accommodate them almost immediately. Her home today is lovelier than ever, filled as it is with husband, pets, and a backyard alive with wildlife. Her sofas, chairs, drapes, and rugs are all in earth tones, bold patterns, and bright prints chosen for their power to disguise stains and animal hair. Her lifestyle actually took her design style beyond control to sanctuary, to a home that reflects that. And so can yours.

Your Personal Color Palette

Open your *Emotional House Design Binder* and pull out the color swatches of your personal color palette from the MY STYLE section. You gathered these on your field trip in the Possessing Personal Style exercises. Now let's see how they apply to and fit into your life.

You separated your color chips into categories that most resembled the primary and secondary colors on the color wheel. Do you remember which were your most prominent colors? The left side has the warm colors. The right side has the cool colors. How many have you chosen from each color group?

Red	# _____		Blue	# _____
Orange	# _____		Green	# _____
Yellow	# _____		Violet	# _____

Scientifically, colors have different properties. Their wavelengths and vibrations differ. Red, for instance, has a longer wavelength than blue, just as hot things have longer wavelengths than cold things, which is why red is considered a warmer color than blue.

Remember, red, orange, and yellow are considered warm colors, while blue, green, and violet are cooler colors. That is because blue, green, and violet have shorter wavelengths. Putting color in your home with this in mind can help you create a therapeutically positive environment designed just for you.

Review the list of negatives below and circle any of the emotional words that apply to you. Be very honest with yourself. This is not deny-who-you-are time. This is for you.

Much of the time I feel very:

Depressed • Angry • Hateful • Sad • Manic • Panicked

Frightened • Exhausted • Unhappy • Distant • Distracted

Reckless • Aggressive • Unmotivated • Alienated

Unconfident • Indecisive • Scattered

Go through your circled list above and pick the three emotions that most adversely affect your life today. Write them below in the order of importance. Put the one you feel the most strongly about at the top and move down from there.

1. _____

2. _____

3. _____

Now that you've acknowledged your areas of emotional imbalance, you are going to address them with color therapy. By injecting color into your home with mood elevators and suppressors, you can take one *design-oriented* step toward dealing with negative feelings.

Color Therapy

Can color affect your mood? Yes. Is it any wonder that institutional green is so commonly found in mental institutions and police stations, where heightened emotional states flourish? Just imagine these same environments painted a fiery red. Would a rehabilitation area or booking room painted red seem right? The color wouldn't go with the function of the space, would it?

The educational system is constantly experimenting with the use of color to enhance concentration, lower absentee rates, and boost morale and performance. Advertisers have also long employed color's power to grab consumers' attention or sway their thinking about a product. Even traffic specialists use the power of color. Why do you think stop signals are red? Red is an assertive color that advances toward you instead of receding away from you. Interior decorators use this knowledge of advancing and receding colors when designing spaces to help give the impression of spacious rooms or cozy spaces.

So yes, indeed, color will affect your mood and even sometimes your physical condition. Pumpkin orange walls are not necessarily a sleep inducer in a bedroom. And blue walls are believed to be an appetite suppressant in the dining room—possibly something to consider if you're dieting. Red is a stimulating color, which enhances sociability. If you prefer a low temperature for sleeping, a bedroom with cool greens or blues can be beneficial. But color is more personal that just the design basics. Everyone is an individual, so you should choose your colors to de-stress your energy level, support your personality, balance your off-kilter emotional states, and bring harmony to your visual experience.

Did you choose the following words?

Aggressive • Angry • Distracted • Hateful

Manic • Panicked • Reckless • Scattered

If so, you'll want to consider using cooler colors in areas of your home where you tend to spend large amounts of time. If you're excitable and anxious, the type who "runs hot," you need cooler, soothing colors to balance you and move you to a more reflective state. Fiery reds and energetic yellows will only stir you up more. Look to grounding colors like brown or green, or use soothing neutrals like beige, or a cool blue in the study or bedroom to invoke the calming influence of the sea. Putting two cool colors together as a color scheme creates a crisper, cleaner look in a room, which might help center those who feel distracted and scattered.

Or did you choose the following emotions?

Alienated • Depressed • Distant • Exhausted • Frightened

Indecisive • Sad • Unconfident • Unhappy • Unmotivated

In this case, you'll want to bring warmer colors into your home. If you lack confidence or feel disconnected, aloof, wiped out, or isolated, warmer hues can help balance you. A warmer color can also help console you when you are frightened, making you feel held and comforted. Look to red-orange hues, rusts, and yellows that will stir your blood, inject some fire into your confidence, warm the cockles of your heart, and reconnect you to the excitement of living.

As you go down your list of three emotions, you can start to see opportunities to create a color scheme based on what you need emotionally. Draw on different combinations from each of the beneficial colors—and the myriad of other colors made from these combinations, like avocado, teal, or lavender—while paying attention to your emotional color needs. Make a note to use these beneficial colors in your EMOTIONAL ROLLER COASTER ROOMS. Jot the color choices in the pertinent ROOM sections of your *Emotional House Design Binder*.

How to Create a Color Scheme

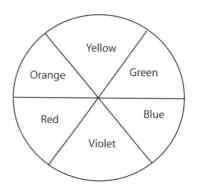

There are several generally accepted formulas for creating a color scheme for your home. Here are the three most common:

The first is called the *complementary* color scheme because it uses complementary colors on the color wheel. This is usually a bold statement. Complementary colors lie directly opposite each other (diagonally across) on the color wheel. Violet and yellow, for instance. Red and green. Or orange and blue. When these combinations are made, each color really pops out at you, which means it seems bolder and more vibrant than it would appear alone or in another color combination. They say opposites attract, but in this case the two colors are "complimenting" each other so vigorously that they both end up a little overflattered. Complementary colors work well for accent pieces or flower gardens, but they can really rev you up emotionally if offered in large quantities, like on walls and floors.

The second color scheme is *analogous*, which uses colors that lie directly *next* to each other on the color wheel; we'll call them neighboring colors: blue and violet; red and orange; red and violet; orange and yellow; yellow and green; and green and blue. This color scheme is very agreeable to the eye because each color has a little bit of the other in it. It feels compatible—the way people who have been together for a long time begin to grow together and sometimes even look alike. Use an analogous color scheme, add a splash of a complementary accent (in art, fabrics, pillows, and accessories), and you have a great color scheme.

The third is the *monochromatic* color scheme, which is created with just one color but in varying shades, tints, and tones. A shade is a color with a just little black added. A tint is a color with a just little white added to it. A tone is a color with a little gray added. Pink is a tint of red, for instance. Maroon is a shade, and dusty rose is a tone. So a red monochromatic color scheme would have several variations of red in darker and lighter saturations. You'll often see a monochromatic color scheme used with neutrals—like beige, bone, and brown. In some ways, it is like your eye is sweeping over the same color as the light shifts through the room, casting shadows here and there.

The monochromatic color scheme can be quite interesting and restful in a very controlled, stylized way. Add an accent of color or black or white to complete the look. If you prefer a deliberate look to your design, a monochromatic color scheme will achieve that.

Old Dogs and New Tricks

Don't think you are too old or too set in your ways to make changes in your environment. It's never too late to bring color into your life. Dotty, a frail senior in her seventies, lived in a house painted all white, both inside and outside, for her entire adult life. Even though she had the exterior recently repainted (white), the interior white walls of her home had grayed with age and become drab and tired. After a difficult surgery, which almost resulted in her relocating to a nursing facility, she decided she needed a fresh coat of interior paint. With a little encouragement, she took the leap, rejected white for the first time, and selected peach as her new wall color. Her disposition brightened instantly and the effect was immediately evident. In her words, "I don't know why, it just makes me happy." Is it any surprise? Peach is a tint of orange, a warm color known for its genial nature. Even the slightest amount of warmth in her home's color brought her good cheer

Back on her feet, she went on to make over her whole house with new flooring, bathroom tiling, carpets, and more. She now has a fresh lease on life. Can color affect your mood? You bet it can.

The Emotional Characteristics of Color

Red—passionate   Orange—genial   Yellow—energetic

Green—balanced   Blue—serene   Violet—visionary

Mauve—ethereal   Pink—whimsical   Beige—receptive

Brown—grounded   Black—absorbing   White—restrained

Color Sentiments

BEIGE is a neutral that neither threatens nor commits, and provides the foundation for a multitude of color schemes. But alone, it is merely a door ajar. If your whole color scheme rests on beige, you are a person who has classic tastes and usually plays it safe. You might want to look at chucking the decorum a little and taking a shot at that long-lost dream you've buried. Start by bringing some bold accents into your home. Splashes of red, black, and orange all marry happily with beige. Injecting your home with color will help to start that motor—it just needs a little gas.

BLACK is unique in that it doesn't reflect light. Worn on the body, it has come to symbolize the elegant, the somber, and the avant-garde. Black will absorb light, which makes it great for nightclubs that want to direct the focus to a lit stage. But on your walls at home it is downright depressing, especially if the finish is flat. On the other hand, highly polished, black lacquered furniture can be quite arresting, although there is a coldness to it, as there is to black leather sofas. In small doses, a glossy black has a glamour about it, but when it overwhelms, the room can become morose and lifeless. Black is a marvelous color for framing, however, because it leaves the image alone and draws your eye in to the artwork.

WHITE is at once devoid of hue and all the colors combined into one. It is often considered pure, and with it comes the sense of purity. But it can also be rather strident and sometimes sterile, which is why you see it in so many hospitals. Worn on the body, white will draw attention—but to the clothing, not to the person wearing it. On your walls, it is no statement at all. It's a blank slate that awaits large and colorful artworks. White is softened and much more agreeable when even tiny quantities of pink, blue, or yellow are added.

YELLOW is a warm color, perhaps because it is the color of golden sunlight. It is an action color—full of optimism and stimulation. Bright lemon yellow can be grating when used in design, but the more muted variations can soothe and hold you, while allowing a gentle warmth to flow over you. Wearing yellow gives off a sense of being gregarious with a sunny disposition. On your walls, yellow is certainly a beam of summer sunshine. The color got a bad rap decades ago when it was believed to cause depression, but today a whole batch of new tones and tints have emerged, offering a warm and happy character.

GREEN is considered a quiet, gentle color, but it all depends on the tint. While green is the stuff of nature and can thrill your eyes in the garden, it takes on a whole new dimension in the home. Use it judiciously, especially in carpeting. A carpet of green grass may be relaxing in your front yard, but inside, the same color on your floor can look like bad Astroturf. It is said that people who wear green tend to be earthy and hardworking. On the walls, green evokes a sense of calm and balance. But the changing saturation levels of green can really change the vibe. While hunter green is a definitively levelheaded color, a pale sage green can seem almost inconsequential. People tend to have strong feelings about green, either positive or negative, but marry it with cool blue and a little white and you instantly have a very relaxing country Cape color scheme.

PINK is pure whimsy—full of carefree play and castles in the air. It's a rather excitable color. There is nothing terribly dire or serious about pink. Perhaps that's why so many young girls have their room painted in this hue. Pink has experienced a real resurgence ever since the *Legally Blonde* movies became big hits with audiences. Many a young girl now associates pink with girl power, as did defiantly feminine fashion queen Coco Chanel many years ago. But pink is not for girls alone. Paired with black, it also offers a Pacific Rim flair. It has an even subtler effect when paired with gray. If you have a frenetic personality, pink will only wind you up more. Manic personalities should stay away from pink. But if you feel sluggish and isolated, a few splashes of it here and there can really perk up a mood. Start with flowers as accents before leaping into a whole room of pink, unless you can keep up with the excitement.

VIOLET (or purple) is a strong, exciting, and ever-so-royal hue. Those who wear it on the body are self-assured, assertive, confident. Those who so paint their walls are unafraid, not easily intimidated, and not to be crossed. In the garden, violet will stop you with an astonished "oh!" In your home, it will make your rooms buzz with bravado. Violet is not a color to be taken lightly. It is the color of kings, priests, and the war-wounded. It is also associated with the occult. (But tell that to a garden iris.) Even though violet lies on the cool side of the color chart, in saturated tones it can be a bold, aggressive statement. Lightened with white into a tint like lavender, it loses its voice instantly. But paint your walls in full saturation and violet will shout out royally to you every day—so be prepared to bow to it.

BLUE is as cool as a winter's day, although it's usually associated with the sea and sky. Blue is the favorite color of Americans, but fares much lower on the preference scale in other nations. Blue is not a threatening color. On the body, blue says "I conform." Just think of the traditional dark blue executive suit or the more commonplace denim jeans. On your walls, a light blue will soothe like a day at the beach. It conveys a sense of tranquility. But go a little darker, and a deep navy hue will pull you into the unfathomable mysteries of the ocean bottom. From space, our planet is a revolving ball of blue. No wonder this color is so popular. Use it for breezy or contemplative environments. It is said to diminish appetite.

BROWN simply has gravitas. It is a solid color, grounded and steady. Worn on the body, brown can seem ill-fitting, bland, and dull, but in rich textures like leather or corduroy, or in combination with cream or rust, it can give a feeling of pluck and a strong sense of self. Similarly, a deep chocolate brown on the walls is a secure statement, at once dramatic and warm. Brown is the color of the solid earth we tread, the invigorating coffee we imbibe, and the delicious chocolate we savor. These are all very safe, comforting things, and this rich color will bestow that same feeling in your home. But used too much and without contrast, it can quickly become dreary and uninteresting.

RED has long been thought of as the color of passion. It is a hot, energetic color, full of excitement and promise. People who wear red aren't afraid to say, "Look at me, I'm here!" On walls or floors, red says that your home is filled with enthusiasm for life. All are welcome, but expect to engage in lively discourse.

The Accent Wall

For those afraid to commit to a whole new color scheme, there's always the accent wall. Remember, nothing is forever—and paint is fast, easy, and changeable. Start with just one wall. Instead of buying a gallon of paint, buy a quart. It'll cost less than $10 and your whole world may change. Latex paint cleans up with water. Oil requires thinner and a more complicated cleanup system. After painting your accent wall, live with the results a while before deciding if you want to go further.

If you are at a loss for how to design your color scheme, you can also use the colors in treasured artworks to define your room's color palette. Check through your existing belongings. Do you already own large pieces with color—a good rug, dominating art piece, or large sofa with a strong pattern? If so, create your color palette with harmonizing colors from these pieces. It will help pull the room together. Choose a main color for the walls that takes a neutral position on these items, then add accent color with drapes, lamps, furnishings, or paint that matches well with the dominant color. Finally, add bold splashes of color with decorative pieces to make your palette sing. These colors can show up in an accent wall or in accessories and plants.

Some things to think about:

- What mood do you want to portray in this room?

- Are the colors complementary or are they analogous or monochromatic combinations?

- Is one of your favorite colors present somewhere in the room?

- Do the colors of walls or furniture in here limit your lifestyle in any way?

The White Cross All Renters Bear

Renters with a difficult landlord—and who hasn't had one—have to deal with the burden of a person who wants your business but also makes it their right to tell you how you must live on their property. You should always try negotiating painting with a landlord before doing it. Their main concerns are the cost of repainting when you move and possible paint damage to hardwood floors, carpeting, or windows. Colored walls are more expensive to repaint than white, because they take more coats to cover and often require an extra primer coat. Most apartments are painted an eggshell white, and by purchasing some primer and a few gallons of the original color in advance for repainting, you might be able to convince the landlord to let you take action. Also, purchasing large drop cloths and painter's blue tape to cover vulnerable areas will help.

If the landlord remains adamant, there are other ways to add color to your rooms. Buy large pre-made canvases and paint them the dominant wall color you would have chosen. Hang them in patterns across your wall so they dominate the white background. The great thing about this option is that you can now carry your portable wall color with you to your next apartment without the expense of painting your new residence. You can also use fabrics, plants, and art to bring in color. The goal is always to inject emotionally balancing color into your life, not fight with a landlord who will always ultimately win.

Remember that unattractive room you made note of in your HOTSPOTS? It's time to revisit it again with color. You're going to create a color palette for this unattractive room. Pick an emotionally beneficial color from the Color Therapy exercise you just did and use it as your dominant color for this room. Next, decide on a color scheme—complementary, analogous, or monochromatic. Using the scheme as a guide, choose secondary and accent colors to go with the main color. Make sure these color chips are already in your color palette pack, so you know you'll be living with colors you love. Place the paint chips for your color scheme in your *Emotional House Design Binder* in the ROOM section for this unattractive room. When you go to redo this room and turn it from an eyesore into a healing space, your color palette and scheme are ready to be put into action with furnishings, fabrics, paint, and accessories.

Paint Touch-Ups

Whenever you paint a room, keep a record of the kind of paint you used and its color code number in your *Emotional House Design Binder*. It's best to keep a color chip and write the name of the paint store on it. When you want to do touch-ups or freshen your paint later, it's important to know if you used a water-based or oil-based paint. It will determine the kind of paintbrush you use and whether you clean up with water or mineral spirits. Jot down the following information to remind yourself later.

PAINT:

Oil or Latex _____   Paint Store _____

Color Name _____   Room Painted _____

Color Code _____   Date Painted _____

HOUSE RULE #12
A Room of One's Own for Everyone—Including Pets

Make sure there is a private, personal space for everyone, even pets.

Virginia Woolf wrote about it in 1929: one needs "a room of one's own" to develop the mind, possess a sense of personal freedom and responsibility, and nurture independent achievement. Not everyone has enough rooms in their home to provide one for every woman, man, and child living in their house, but you can mark off a separate *space* for everyone, even if it's just a corner, a nook, or a section of a room that belongs to them alone.

A space of one's own means multifunctioning your space while keeping privacy in mind (like with a room divider). No one wants to be on display in their private space—they want privacy. That way they can keep it as messy or neat as they want, without disturbing common space, and they can engage in solitary activities without inviting curious eyes.

"Everyone" really does mean everyone. Mom needs private space, but she shouldn't get to appropriate the bedroom if she shares that with Dad. Dad needs private space, but he shouldn't be able to take possession of the family room, banishing everyone else to their bedrooms. Kids need private space as soon as they're old enough; audio-based monitors can keep an ear to the door until a certain agreed-upon age. Older kids should be allowed private time without monitoring—but they shouldn't be allowed to take over the whole house. Learning to be alone is an important part of developing maturity, a strong relationship with oneself, and self-comforting techniques.

Even pets need a space of their own. Animals naturally create dens and nests, and you need to honor those instincts: they have emotional needs just like we do. They need a place to retreat that is theirs alone, a place that is safe from interference by other pets, kids, or an oblivious adult. Not a chair that you might sit in or your bed that you might kick them off of. But a doggie bed, a cat perch, or a hamster hideaway tunnel—even fish in an aquarium need plant life or a cave that gives them a place to hide.

Birds naturally retreat to the trees for cover when they sleep, and they will be healthier, happier birds if that environment is re-created for them—so cover their cages at night. If you have multiple pets, each one needs a bed, den, nest, or habitat that suits their size.

Don't desert your Emotional House elements or the Four Cornerstones—harmony, balance, support, and a stress-free environment. Apply all of the House Rules to any private space to make it work. (Even pets have an aesthetic: mimic a natural setting or match bedding color to their fur like camouflage.)

Sad Dogs and Englishwomen

Some time ago, a single female client inherited a second dog. Her first, Robbie, was a sweet old sheepdog mix that had been rescued and was very sensitive to abandonment and threats to his turf. The second arrived on scene, a middle-aged Yorkshire terrier named Bart, who had been pawned off on her by an acquaintance who had largely neglected him. Bart was used to not being alpha, but you could see his sadness when he had to back off while Robbie hogged their lady's lap. We suggested she could reassure Bart with a bed of his own and picked one up for her from a local pet store. It matched Bart's coloring *and* blended with her home's color palette. Bart took to it in a heartbeat. Robbie was suspicious, but it was too small for him and he left it alone soon enough.

At last report, Bart is still going straight to it whenever Robbie turfs the little Yorkie from their owner's lap and anytime a visitor comes in, whether that person makes him nervous or calm. At night, when they all head for bed, Robbie follows his missus to the bedroom, and Bart trundles off to his own little bed, his tiny tail wagging . . . and he's still there when she wakes up in the morning.

We don't think people are any different from little Bart. Everyone is happier when they have a spot they can rely on, a place to go to that is theirs and theirs alone. It relieves stress, gives you a spot where you can rebalance and allows you a place for the personal time everyone needs to grow and plan their future in a physically supportive way—three very important Emotional House Program cornerstones.

Who's Responsible? or
"Ain't Nobody's Business If I Do ..."

Whether it's a grand study, a workshop in the garage, or a comfy chair with a reading light by a bay window, your private space has to be taken care of. Who else would you want to do this thing? Most people develop "just so" opinions about their favorite private things. Even a three-year-old will exclaim, "Not on my toy box!" when Daddy attempts to put her cowboy boots down for the night. If you're paying attention, that's a child who is amenable to taking responsibility for her own space.

Anyone who has strict standards for their personal space needs to take responsibility for maintaining it, at least insofar as they communicate these standards clearly to a housekeeper, if not altogether by doing the dusting, straightening, and vacuuming themselves. Many people with home offices understand that someone else might throw important papers away without realizing it, or in an organizing effort, "lose" a crucial item in the wrong stack.

Equally, everyone should be allowed to keep their "rooms of their own" to their own standards, even if they're low. If they like clean but wrinkled clothes in a heap, posters of Shrek on the wall, or stacks of books on the floor, it's none of your business as long as they're not violating good health sense. Mess is one thing; dirt, food spills, and wet or soiled clothes are another matter entirely. These will attract problems and create an unhealthy environment—bugs and bacteria—so they must be handled. But one person's treasure trove is another's clutter, and one's neat and orderly is another's uptight and sterile. Common spaces must strike a compromise, but you should have total say over your little piece of earth, even if it's only a chair.

A Note on Teenagers and Privacy

Teenagers, by developmental mandate, are struggling to explore their separateness from the family unit. It's a bit of an understatement to say it can be difficult for everybody ... but they're going to be on their own sooner than anyone would like to think, and it's important that all the little "trial separations" of adolescence proceed in an atmosphere that offers support as well as safety. This hormonally charged time puts teens through such drastic physical, emotional, and mental changes that it's important to respect their need for privacy.

However, because of some very high-profile tragedies caused by some very troubled teens, it's become popular to suggest that parents should make a habit of searching their children's bedrooms and backpacks. Consider this option carefully before you proceed with it. Because, if you're at the point of probing into your kid's things, you've probably been off track with one another for a long time. Communication and trust have already broken down.

Harmony, balance, support, and freedom from stress have long been sacrificed to other principles, whatever they might've been. If danger is imminent, sure, you might have to ransack your kid's room to prevent it. But violating any family member's privacy will only notify you of trouble that you should already be aware of.

There might be better ways to learn about your children's lives and keep them safe in the world than by rummaging through their belongings. Being genuinely interested in their welfare and their concerns and being involved in their lives in a way that gives true support (unremitting criticism is not support, it's disparaging), while involving them in yours, is a more effective way of keeping them away from trouble. This is not to suggest you be their buddy. Having someone interested as a parent, not a buddy or lord and master, is a dream of every child. Keep boundaries in mind when respecting a teenager's right to a room of his or her own.

Creating *Your* Unique "Room of Your Own"

Get out your HOUSE JOURNAL—it's dream and plan time. Answer the following:

1. Which area in your home is your private space and yours alone? _____

2. Does it infringe upon common areas or the rights of other occupants, cutting them off from their emotional or practical needs? _____

3. If you don't have a private space, where can you create one in your home by seizing possession of an unused area or show room or by multifunctioning a common space? _____

Before you decide on the area, review your FIVE-YEAR LIFE PLAN in the GOALS section of your HOUSE JOURNAL to see which personal goals this private area may have to service. It might determine the location and room you'll be multipurposing. You may want this area to service some of those future labels or titles you *want* to own. Or perhaps you just want a spot to read all the great classics undisturbed. It's your space, so make it work for you!

4. What sorts of things will you have in your private space? Make a dream list.

   _____ _____ _____ _____

5. What comfort crutches could you add that would boost your morale and remind you of the beauty of your inner spirit? Make a list.

   _____ _____ _____ _____

6. What organizing items will you need? Make a list.

_____ _____ _____ _____

7. What color theme will enliven you or soothe you here? Name three colors from your personal color palette—a dominant color, a harmonizing color, and an accent color.

- The dominant color will cover the most area (or fabric if it's just a chair)
- A harmonizing color may be another shade or tint of the dominant color or one that neighbors your dominant color on the color wheel.
- A bolder accent color that really pops, possibly a complementary color that is directly opposite your dominant color on the color wheel.

_____ _____ _____ _____

This will be your color scheme for your private space. Keep it in mind when you purchase paint, accessories, and furniture.

8. What kind of art do you want here? Oils, watercolors, needlepoint, sculpture, or another type? Decide on one. _____

9. What divine details will imbue your private space with beauty? Write down two.

_____ _____

10. What furniture and fabrics will be in your private space? Make a list.

_____ _____ _____ _____

11. What are you most looking forward to doing in your private space?

_____

Put this design plan in the HOUSE PLAN section of your *Emotional House Design Binder*, so you don't forget it. And add your shopping list to the ROOM you're going to multifunction. Make sure any partition items you need are on that list. Don't let this commitment to yourself slide. Write the pledge, "I *will* create private space just for me!" in your GOALS section of your HOUSE JOURNAL. Good work! This was a huge step toward creating an Emotional House for yourself. Move on now to Part III, Your House, which begins with A Journey Through Your Home. The physical work is about to begin!

YOUR HOUSE

⚜ { 21 } ⚜

A Journey Through Your Home

Now let's go through *your* house to find the places that don't work because they don't comply with the basic House Rules, as well as the ones that could work better if they improved upon the Four Cornerstones. This will guide you in your plans, showing you what's most crucial, what will take the most commitment in terms of time and money, and what you could do in a free evening for the price of dinner. But first, let's recap what you've learned:

The Building Blocks of Your Emotional House: Recap

The Four Cornerstones

The Four Cornerstones are the keystones buttressing your Emotional House's foundation. They describe the atmosphere you will experience inside an Emotional House:

Harmony • Balance • Support • A Stress-Free Environment

Your Blueprint

Your personal Blueprint (the logistics of your unique life) defines exactly how these corner-stones will be manifested in your design and layout—the one you create for the lifestyle you actually live, and for the person you hope to grow to become. Your Blueprint comprises your factoids, labels, obstacles, goals, your coming attractions, emotional roller coasters, personal style, and your home's HOTSPOTS.

Your Foundation

The Emotional House Foundation is comprised of twelve House Rules. They are the girders that fortify the Four Cornerstones, while ensuring that your personal Blueprint thrives.

The House Rules

Rule #1: Live in Your Whole House

Rule #2: Keep It Clean

Rule #3: Comfort: First and Foremost

Rule #4: Lifestyle Dictates Design Style

Rule #5: A Show House Is No House

Rule #6: A Place for Everything and Everything in Its Place

Rule #7: Art Is Smart

Rule #8: Set Boundaries for Room Use

Rule #9: If It's Broke, Fix It

Rule #10: The Divine Is in the Details

Rule #11: All White Is Not Right

Rule #12: A Room of One's Own for Everyone—Including Pets

You now know that having your design style fit your real lifestyle can create *harmony* both practically and emotionally. You know that maintaining a *balance* in furniture arrangement, complementary design features, and the proper and fair use of space for all provides an atmosphere of emotional balance for everyone. And you know why show rooms are a no-no, unless all the practical and emotional functions needed for a life in balance have been met by the other rooms in your home.

You understand how good boundaries, routine cleanliness, and healthy workable spaces can *support* your daily needs and lend harmony to family interactions. And, you understand how art, color, and divine elements can enliven your senses and support your emotional and intellectual growth.

You also know that you need comfort and beauty items, a clear organizational workflow, everything in working order, and a private area in which to regroup and expand your horizons: to relieve *stress* and support your dreams for the future.

And most importantly, you have a better understanding of how the rooms in your home were originally designed to support all your practical and emotional needs, and that by following the House Rules you will not only return your rooms to their proper state of balance, but elevate them to the level of partner in your process of personal development.

The Practical and Emotional Functions of Each Room

How will the rules do this? By ensuring the right functions are served, and by turning your:

- FOYER into a "gate" to *equalize* your bearings in the *transition* between outside and inside.

- KITCHEN into a "hearth" that provides *physical sustenance* and emotional *nurturance*

- LIVING ROOM into a "tribal council" of *fellowship* where a feeling of *camaraderie* can grow

- DINING ROOM into a "round table" for *communion* and *bonding* with family and others

- BEDROOM into a "sanctuary" for *sleep, solitude, and sex,*
  where *intimacy* is cherished

- BATHROOM into a "temple bath" for the sacred act of
  purification and *reverence* for self

- HOME OFFICE into "central records" for the *business of the family* and personal *accountability*

- BASEMENT/GARAGE into a "keep" where *storage* becomes
  a healing place of *remembrance*

- STUDIO/WORKSHOP into a "labor and delivery room"
  where you give birth to *self-expression* through *creative arts*

- GARDEN into an "Eden" where *cultivation and harvesting*
  enliven a scenic locale of *serenity*

- REC ROOM into a "playhouse" where *fun and fitness*
  provide a *release* from stress

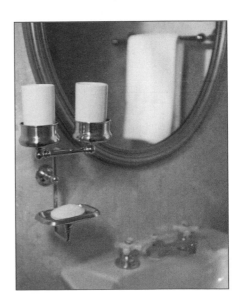

- KIDS' ROOMS into a "fort" where the *hideout* is a safe place for the inner work of *becoming*

- LAUNDRY ROOM into a "river" where *washing and folding* refresh your options and provide *new beginnings*.

The Walk-Through—Your House Checklist

Understanding these Emotional House principles, it's time to do a final walk-through of your home to see how well it measures up to your personal Blueprint, follows the House Rules,

fulfills the practical and emotional functions of each room as it was intended, and ultimately stands up to the Four Cornerstones. Grab your *Emotional House Design Binder* and let's go.

In the list that follows, go through each room and write down the numbers of *any* rules that are broken. You will quickly see where your Emotional House needs work. The rooms with the most broken rules need the most attention and will help you set priorities for change.

12 House Rules Checklist

1. LIVE IN YOUR WHOLE HOUSE.
Are both the emotional and practical functions met? *See the Functions Table in chapter 9.*

2. KEEP IT CLEAN.
Is the room clean, and is there a cleaning schedule to keep it that way?

3. COMFORT: FIRST AND FOREMOST.
Are there two comfort items in this room—and what about comfort crutches?

4. LIFESTYLE DICTATES DESIGN STYLE.
Is there anything here that inhibits or doesn't fit with your true lifestyle?

5. A SHOW HOUSE IS NO HOUSE.
Is the room a seldom-used showplace?

6. A PLACE FOR EVERYTHING AND EVERYTHING IN ITS PLACE.
Is the room well organized?

7. ART IS SMART.
Is there an art piece other than family photos in the room?

8. SET BOUNDARIES FOR ROOM USE.
Have boundaries for usage been set and enforced? Is the room safe and secure?

9. IF IT'S BROKE, FIX IT.
Are any repairs needed?

10. THE DIVINE IS IN THE DETAILS.
Are there two divine beauty elements inside?

11. ALL WHITE IS NOT RIGHT.
Is there coordinated color in this room?

12. A ROOM OF ONE'S OWN FOR EVERYONE.
Do you feel welcome here, and is there a personal space for you here?

Your House Checklist

Foyer _____

Kitchen _____

Pantry _____

Breakfast Nook _____

Dining Room _____

Living Room _____

Family Room/Den _____

Master Bedroom _____

2nd Bedroom _____

Guest Bedroom _____

Kids' Rooms _____

Bathroom _____

Home Office _____

Garden/Yard _____

Laundry Room _____

Basement/Attic _____

Garage _____

Studio/Shop _____

Recreation Room _____

Library _____

Service Quarters _____

Other _____

Other _____

Transfer the list of broken rules to the pertinent ROOM section of your *Emotional House Design Binder*. The actions you need to take in these individual rooms are now much clearer.

Okay, it's time to do a bit of housekeeping. Check in your HOUSE PLAN section for your notes. If there are additional actions, repairs, comfort crutches, or coming attractions that you've already noted, transfer these to their pertinent ROOMS as well. How about treasured items you discovered in the D.U.S.T. exercise in House Rule #2: Keep it Clean (chapter 10)? Are there special places where they'd be more beneficial? If you want to move things into specific rooms, make a note of it now, so you'll have your whole plan in the right ROOM section when you get there.

Picking a Room to Start With

Serious repairs need priority attention to get the bones of your home in working order. But in general, begin with any rooms that break Rule #1 first—rooms that don't fulfill the correct *practical or emotional needs*. If there are several of these rooms, then start with the room that breaks the most rules in addition to Rule #1 and work back from there.

List the rooms that are your three greatest offenders:

1. _____   2. _____   3. _____

All the rules build on each other, just as bricks and mortar do. You might find that by repairing one rule, several others will fall in line like dominoes. For example: Maybe you don't live in your whole house—a violation of Rule #1—because you are maintaining an unused show room—a violation of Rule #5. You may have also come to realize that you are stressed and feel unsupported—a problem with two of your emotional Cornerstones—and the main reason is that there is no personal space for you in your home, a violation of Rule #12: A Room of One's Own for Everyone.

Just by taking over that useless show room and transforming it into a private retreat for yourself, you will have corrected Rules #1, #5, and #12 and reinforced your cornerstones. You will now benefit from a sense of ownership and also have a place of solitude to de-stress and develop strategies that support your personal dreams and goals beyond your daily responsibilities to family and community.

Looking back at the list of your three greatest offenders, jot down some actions you could take to remedy them. For example: clean bathroom, organize kitchen cupboards, hang art, fix leak, paint, multipurpose the living room, add lumbar supports to stiff-backed chairs, convert unused bedroom to art studio, remove carpeting at poolside door and install tile, add cubbies for sports equipment and so on.

Room #1 _____

Room #2 _____

Room #3 _____

Make a note of these decisions in the pertinent ROOM sections of your *Emotional House Design Binder*.

Making Your Plan—An Overview

Now that you've chosen the rooms you want to work on, you need to set your plan in motion. Begin with Room #1 and look closely at your problem for a resolution. For example:

ROOM: Dining room—*The Round Table*

BROKEN RULE: #1—Dining room does not meet proper function

PROBLEM: Room can't serve as place of dining (*communion* and *bonding*) because of paper pileup, laptop, and bills on table

SOLUTION: Create a better-organized home office elsewhere

The resolution lies in finding a proper home for the offending task. Choose a space you can easily multifunction. Let's say you have an unused alcove in the kitchen that has become a dumping ground for everyone's junk. Since you do most of the cooking and accounting, this is a perfect space to multifunction. Invoke Rule #8 on boundaries—and instruct others to remove their junk from the alcove and store it appropriately so you can use that space.

Now you'll create your project plan in four simple steps. Repeat this system for every room in your house. It's the same process, whether you're rearranging furniture, cleaning, reorganizing, multipurposing a space, or doing a total room makeover.

1. Set your goal.

2. Set your budget.

3. Set a time limit.

4. Set a schedule.

> A goal is just a dormant idea without a time limit and a schedule to reach it.

Setting Your Goal

Be specific when setting goals. Start with your main objective and then express your desired aspirations. For example:

MAIN GOAL: Multipurpose kitchen to include an office nook in the alcove

ASPIRATIONS: Adequate privacy, high-speed Internet accessibility, coordination with existing room décor

Now it's your turn. Take a chance and state your main goal for room #1.

My main goal for room #1 is: _____

What are your additional aspirations for this goal? _____

_____

Now that you know what you want to do, you can set your budget for the project.

Setting Your Budget

Don't ever get locked into any change, renovation, or makeover based on a fixed idea of what the project "costs," because costs are entirely adjustable, depending on how you plan your design. Plan around what you can afford, and no more than that—we can't stress this enough. If you experience financial crisis enacting one small change, you'll be less likely to embark on future ones. Don't be swayed by the many temptations out there, especially if incurring unreasonable debt is habitual for you. New desks for that office nook can cost anywhere from $39 to $10,000 plus, so narrow your vision to what is appropriate for your wallet. You want to reach a goal, not strive for some elusive notion of perfection. Recycled demolition materials and even $2 flea market finds can be entirely transformed with a fresh coat of paint or faux finish. Owners of an exclusive shop in Los Angeles have made millions doing this, and their high-end clients don't know the difference.

Beef up your budget by digging out that Yuck Box of unpleasant memorabilia you assembled in the D.U.S.T. exercise in House Rule #2: Keep it Clean (chapter 10). Hold a garage sale, sell that junk, and you've turned your emotional dirt into useful compost—more money for your renovations!

Remember, always state how much your budget is, and where your money will come from, so you can remain realistic about your spending. For example:

TOTAL BUDGET	$500
Available Funds	$410 from savings account
Loaned Funds	$90 on credit card

A credit card is not available money. It is *loaned* money that comes with corresponding financing fees, so treat it accordingly. It's a good idea to decide how long you will carry any debt on your credit cards. Check your interest rates to determine exactly how much the $90 in debt will cost you in its entirety after interest charges. These calculations can be complicated, so go on the Internet where you can access dozens of free credit card interest calculators to help you calculate overall costs. Just type in "credit card interest calculator" in any search engine and a whole stream of websites will come up.

This loan of $90 will take you ten months to pay off if you pay only the minimum payment of $10 a month, with additional loan charges ranging from $6.50 to $8, depending on your interest rate. Understanding and acknowledging the actual debt you are incurring for each charge is a great motivator to pay those cards off in full each month.

ADD A 15% CUSHION TO YOUR BUDGET

It's very difficult to stick to a budget. Even experienced designers struggle with this and advise you to be prepared for 15% in overruns. That's because there are always little things that weren't factored into the original budget. But instead of adding another 15% to your existing budget figure—the one you are already comfortable with—reduce your original number by 15% and make that lower figure your spending budget. Keep the rest as a cushion.

For example: Since you've decided your total budget is $500 for your office nook, your actual *spending budget* should be $425 because you've decreased it by a 15% contingency cushion of $75 for unexpected expenses.

TOTAL BUDGET	$500
Minus 15% Cushion	−75
TOTAL SPENDING BUDGET:	$425

This same formula applies whether you are tackling a big or small job. If you have a total of $100 budgeted, your spending budget should be $85 with a $15 contingency cushion. If you have a total budget of $10,000, your spending budget should be $8,500 with a 15% cushion of $1,500.

Always plan for and shop for the lower figure (the spending budget), and you'll have a better chance of staying within your total budget. Later, when you discover that you need an extra coat of paint, hinges for your wall divider, file folders for your new filing cabinet, or a footstool, and you forgot to enter your $8 credit card interest charge, you'll be covered.

People doing major renovations frequently forget to factor in costs like building permits, utility hookups, interim storage and packing boxes, temporary housing, and subcontractor and loan fees.

How much could you realistically afford to budget now for your main goal for room #1?

MY TOTAL BUDGET $ _____

MY SPENDING BUDGET: $ _____

Setting Your Time Limit

Setting a specific time for your project's beginning is the fastest way to propel your goal from the dormant state to an active stage.

Things to take into consideration when setting your time limit include:

- **Sketching out a floor plan** (the same applies if you are just reorganizing)

- **Consulting home repair manuals** (to review materials and labor involved)

- **Pricing your raw materials, tool rentals, furnishings, and accessories**

- **Getting bids if you decide to hire a contractor or a designer**

- **Shopping, cleaning, organizing, rearranging, repair, or construction time**

Set your time limit using two parameters:

1. **The total length of time it will take to complete your goal** (for example, 4 days)

2. **The starting date and ending date** (for example, two consecutive weekends, starting July 23rd and finishing July 31st)

Immediately mark those dates on your calendar. Now you know you cannot accept dinner invitations or attend parties on those dates. You have a goal you are going to achieve!

THE DIY ROUTE (DO-IT-YOURSELF)

If you go the DIY route—doing it yourself—be prepared for the fact that no renovation goes without a hitch. If you tear up floors, you may find rotten boards or termites underneath. Tear out a wall, and there's decrepit electrical wiring or failing plumbing that needs updating. Behind the skin of the walls, floors, and ceilings, your home hides its dirty little secrets. If you are prepared for some hitches before you start, you won't be blindsided when they occur.

Always buy the best raw materials you can afford. "All wood" products are always preferable over particleboard or MDF (medium density fiberboard) for an Emotional House. MDF is constructed with a resin that contains urea formaldehyde. If you do use MDF in your home, always paint all areas to ensure that any toxicity is contained, and when cutting or sanding MDF, use a ventilator and protective eyewear.

> ### TOOL RENTAL WAIVER INSURANCE
>
> Spring for the extra insurance when renting tools. Unfamiliar tools can easily be damaged by new users, and replacements are pricey!

THE REALITY OF USING CONTRACTORS

Remember, if your goal involves employing a contractor, call and get estimates for how long the job will take, then *double* their ballpark figure and adjust your dates accordingly. Contractors are notorious for underestimating job length and often will slip in other jobs while doing yours. This invariably happens in spite of your numerous objections. Expect to find yourself placing calls asking where the subcontractors are and why they haven't shown up at the designated time, and finally throwing your arms up, screaming, "How can they possibly make a living this way?" Don't take it personally, it seems it's just the nature of the beast.

Get three bids before assigning a job to a professional. Look at portfolios, check licenses and insurance bonds, and pick the contractor you like. But if the contractor or designer you're considering isn't available on your scheduled dates, move on to someone else. Don't let your goal be delayed by someone else's busy schedule.

What is your:

Total length of time to complete your first goal? _____

Starting date? _____

Completion date? _____

Now that you have your dates, mark them on your calendar. Immediately apply for a building permit if you need one and book your workers—family, friends, or professionals.

Setting Your Schedule

Congratulations, you have now selected a room you are going to fix. You have a main goal for this room. You've set a budget for how much you are going to spend, and you've decided how long it will take and, most importantly, *when* you will start. It's time to set your schedule of activities and make your TO DO list. Start simply, with broad strokes. For example:

1st WEEKEND   July 23rd—Measure, make floor plan, make shopping & TO DO lists. Shop.

                       July 24th—Paint and finish any shopping left to do.

2nd WEEKEND   July 30th—Build wall divider and run computer cable.

                       July 31st—Arrange furniture. Set up files and hook up computer.

Take a running start at making your schedule for your first goal right now. Don't worry if it's not perfect; you can adjust it all later.

Date: _____   To Do: _____

Date: _____   To Do: _____

Date: _____   To Do: _____

Date: _____   To Do: _____

Great. Now make your shopping list, keeping your *spending* budget in mind.

Your Shopping List

Make two lists: your MUST HAVES—the essentials, like a gallon of paint, a desk and a chair, and organizing items; then, your WISH LIST—the little extras that you could live without but would love to have, like two phone lines with a dual answering machine and caller ID.

Shop for the MUST HAVES first. Don't dip into your 15% cushion fund until the whole job is done. A sample shopping list for the office nook project would be:

MUST HAVES	WISH LIST
Desk with a drawer	Second phone line
Task chair & lamp	Two-line answering machine w/caller ID
Filing cabinet	Accounting software
Plywood, hinges & fabric for partition	Wireless Internet router
Cable for Internet hookup	Lumbar support

Look back at any of the initial shopping lists you made in your ROOM sections in the *Emotional House Design Binder* as you went through the workbook. Reassess those lists now and divide them into your MUST HAVES and WISH LIST. Then, make your new list for your current goal:

MUST HAVES	WISH LIST
_____	_____
_____	_____
_____	_____
_____	_____

You finally have all the things you need to set your plan in motion: a goal, budget, time limit, schedule, and rudimentary TO DO and shopping lists. You've booked your dates and your workers, gotten any permits you may need, and are ready to launch your plan into action.

As you shop, mark down the cost of each item and add it up to see how each purchase affects your overall spending budget. Adjust your selections as you go, making sure you stick to your final figure as you move through your shopping list. If, for instance, there's no money left for that art object you wanted, consider creative options. Use the Fashioning Your Anchor exercise from chapter 15 to make your own inspirational art piece using left-over paint and elements from your goal picture board to inspire you.

Going Through the Fire

Every project, no matter how big or how small, will come to a point where you want to give up. This is when you have to dig down and *go through the fire* to complete the project. View this as a life test. It is a measure of your resolve to improve your life. When you hit these roadblocks, take a moment to remind yourself of exactly why you started the project in the first place by answering these three questions:

What will my life be like if I stop now? _____

_____

How will I feel whenever I enter this room as it is now? _____

_____

How will my life improve if I *go through the fire* to reach my goal? _____

_____

Keep your main goal alive as a motivator. After it's done, you will not only feel great in that room, but you will have the satisfaction of having reached a goal you personally designed to improve your life. That's worth the sweat!

Measure for Measure—Preparing for Change

You're almost ready to begin the final chapters and change your home into an Emotional House. But before you launch into redoing your rooms, measure everything so you can make a floor plan and ensure everything will fit properly. A common mistake when ordering new furniture and floor coverings is buying furnishings that are either too large for a room or too small. Showrooms are large spaces that can easily fool the eye in terms of scale. You must take length, width, and height of your room into account when installing new items, especially large-scale furnishings like bookshelves and armoires, which look heavy and crowded in rooms with low ceilings. Conversely, if you have soaring ceilings, small furnishings can appear dwarfed. Measure all your rooms now or, at the very least, do them as you go along.

Room Measurements

Start by measuring the rooms and windows. Indicate the areas where the doors and windows are located and the floor area where the door sweeps open (you can't place furniture there). If you didn't get your graph paper when you made your *Emotional House Design Binder*, get some now. Use one piece of graph paper per room. Store your measurements in the pertinent ROOM section.

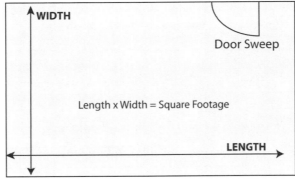

To get a room's square footage, multiply the room's length X its width. Do not include the height.

Window Measurements

Measure the height and width of all the windows next. Keep these measurements in your ROOM sections for future use as well. Window treatments can hang inside your windows, exposing the trim molding, or outside of the window, covering the trim, depending on personal preference.

To "cheat the size" of a small window, use the outer mount measurement and hang floor-length curtains, providing a more dramatic effect. In this case be sure to measure the height of the wall, too.

Use outer measurement to hide trim molding. Use inner measurement to expose trim molding.

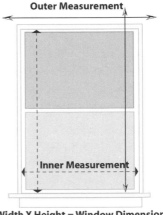

Width X Height = Window Dimension

Furniture Measurements

Finally, measure all your existing furniture—height, width, and depth—so you can prepare floor plans. This is important. You will regret it if your new high-definition television won't slip into that old armoire, if you can't get the new fridge through a doorway, or if your new linens are too small for your new bed with the extra plush pillowtop. Keep your measurements in the pertinent ROOM section of your *Emotional House Design Binder*.

These will come in handy for years to come. You may change residences, but you usually haul your old furniture with you. It all may even become handy in an insurance claim. Here's a sample of the type of information you'll want to record:

Armoire:

Length	_____	Depth Inside	_____
Width	_____	Make & Finish	_____
Height	_____	Date purchased	_____

DVD Player:

Length	_____	Serial #	_____
Width	_____	Model	_____
Height	_____	Warranty Yrs.	_____

Making Your Floor Plan Mock-Ups

After all your measurements are compiled, use your graph paper to create mini paper cutouts of your rooms and furniture to scale. Let each square on the graph paper equal 6 inches (15 cm). Rearranging scaled cutouts on your floor layouts is far easier than moving furniture. Shuffle your pieces around like game pieces on a Scrabble board. Sometimes outstanding solutions will appear from a random shuffle. When you get an arrangement you like, use a glue stick or tape to secure the pieces and create a floor plan. Add them to the pertinent ROOM in your *Emotional House Design Binder*.

Coordinating Your Look and Design

Use the floor plan mock-ups to create a design board like designers do. Add magazine clippings you've collected in your INSPIRATION section and color schemes and design choices from the MY STYLE section of your *Emotional House Design Binder*. Add your paint chips, fabric swatches, and photographs of furniture to get the overall look before you make permanent alterations. Now's the time to see if that paint really matches that upholstery, if curtains clash with rugs, if art complements the room function, and if there's enough room to maneuver around comfortably. Adjustments are easier at the planning stage. Sometimes a slight change in color tint or flooring can make all the difference.

Good work! Now it's time to tackle those rooms for real. You know which room you are going to start with, so begin your process by asking these three questions for the room first.

1. Where are my HOTSPOTS in this room?

2. Is this an EMOTIONAL ROLLER COASTER ROOM for me?

3. Are there COMING ATTRACTIONS I need to prepare for in this room?

Address the issues in that order. And if the room *is* an EMOTIONAL ROLLER COASTER ROOM for you, engage in the D.U.S.T. exercise immediately. Look for any emotional dirt lingering here, either in the room's possessions or in your memories of long-ago events that took place in this kind of room. Be gentle with yourself and add "Comfort Crutches" immediately. As you approach each of the rooms that follow, remember the building blocks of an Emotional House and apply these concepts to yours. Equally important, have fun!

❧{ 22 }❧

Foyer

THE GATE

PRACTICAL FUNCTION	EMOTIONAL FUNCTION
Transition	Equalizing

Your Gate

The entryway's importance should not be underestimated—it is where you are received every time you arrive home. Your front hall has a very specific *transitional* function: it's a bridge between the outside world and your inner sanctum. It brings outsiders to the point where they are approved and invited in, or dispatched with in short order. More to the point, it welcomes you in from the cold, cruel world and braces you again when you head out.

The emotional function of the foyer is to *equalize* your comings and goings. If you've ever sensed an uncomfortable pressure in your ears as you dropped in elevation—as during an airplane's descent—you've recognized your body's attempt to adjust your internal pressure to the sudden change in atmosphere. Once your ears pop, you feel fine again. Entering your home after a long, hard day works pretty much the same way. You exhale with relief as you equalize your system to the home atmosphere of safety and comfort. This is why the foyer is important. If, when you arrive home, you are greeted by a riot of shoes and hockey equipment you must maneuver around, or a tumble of wet umbrellas and cast-off clothing that blocks your access, your pressure doesn't equalize to a place of comfort, but rather, increases. And that makes for a rocky reentry.

The environment and décor of your entryway is truly a barometer of the atmosphere that lies ahead. Is yours a warm welcome or a chaotic reception? Does it act like a good "butler," helping you to dispense with—and retrieve—keys, outerwear, umbrella, and mail? Does it help you feel put together and ready to greet the world that awaits you? To elevate this area to Emotional House standards, make the adjustments needed for a transitional space.

RULES OF THE ROOM

1. Adjustable lighting (dimmers) to ease vision from exteriors to interiors.

2. Console or bench to hold personal items.

3. Framed mirror near door to check on your personal presentation.

4. Coat rack, hangers, or hooks to contain outerwear.

5. Drip mat or absorbent rug to control exterior debris.

6. An outdoor transitional component: flowers or full-spectrum lighting.

Coming In Out of the Rain

You want your foyer to generate a harmonious, balanced, supportive, and stress-free experience the minute you walk through the door. If instead you feel instantly lonely as you enter your home, or find yourself tensing up, suddenly yelling, or just feeling like you want to turn around and leave again, then your foyer is not working to bring you home. Instead it is an EMOTIONAL ROLLER COASTER area in your home. Go through every House Rule and make changes in this room! Decide: What is the first thing you want to feel when you come home? And what do you want others to know or feel when they enter? Answering these questions will give you your foyer's theme.

A Swingin' Gate

EASY ON THE EYES: Adjustable full-spectrum lighting eases vision from exteriors to interiors.

DECON ZONE: Umbrella stands & mats for muddy shoes slough off the outer world's effects.

THANK YOU, JEEVES: A sturdy spot to rest keys, bags, or purses keeps passages clear and clean.

KEEP IT REAL: No teetering fake wall tables, priceless breakables, or delicate pieces in the foyer.

SHOE CLUTTER: Combat shoe clutter with ascending step-like risers & shoe racks.

HANG IT UP: Extra hooks, coat racks & hangers are a message to visitors that they're welcomed.

OPEN 24 HOURS: There's *no* security if keys are left under mats or plants or above ledges at doors.

SAFE AND SOUND: House keys kept near doors should be in an enclosure inaccessible to visitors.

ODD NOOKS & CRANNIES: Foyers are perfect spots for useful extra storage units & baskets.

OUTSIDE, INSIDE: Fresh flowers & floral art promote transition between the two areas.

THE EVIL EYE: Portraits in the foyer are too imposing for the equalizing function of this area.

PASSWORD, PLEASE: Secret family passwords give children the edge with strangers trying to enter.

COMING TOGETHER: A color analogous to the next visible room's dominant color unifies a theme.

PERCHING POST: Give messengers & tradespeople a bench to wait on to keep them in place at the door.

ART DICTATES BEHAVIOR: A poster of dogs playing poker in the foyer says, "Anything goes here!"

AN ICY RECEPTION: Keep a can of lock de-icer in the car in areas with harsh winters.

MIRROR, MIRROR ON THE WALL: The foyer's focal point should be directly opposite the door.

LOCK IT UP: Deadbolts, supplemental chain locks & peepholes are a must on all entry doors.

A NEW TRADITION—CREATING A TOUCHSTONE

If you don't already have a feel-good ritual when you come in, you need one. Pick an item in the foyer to act as your touchstone. Whenever you enter your house, take off your coat and hat, kick off your shoes, and put your keys and burdens where they belong, take a moment to just lay a hand on your touchstone and impart a silent message to yourself that you are home. Your touchstone may be a stairway finial, a railing, a wind chime, a favorite sculpture, or a traditional form in the doorway that you tap every time you come or go. Whatever you choose, it will act as a visceral message to your soul that you have refuge here.

❦ 23 ❦

Living Room

THE TRIBAL COUNCIL

PRACTICAL FUNCTION	EMOTIONAL FUNCTION
FELLOWSHIP & ENTERTAINMENT	CAMARADERIE

Your Tribal Council

The need for belonging on the soul level is woven into the very fabric of our DNA, going back to the time we lived in tribes. We need a space that offers a simple place for being together, and this is the modern-day living room—your "tribe's" council where all relationships are developed—family, friends, and romantic. And this is the room where the issues you have with groups are written all over it.

If this is an EMOTIONAL ROLLER COASTER ROOM for you—if you have issues with belonging, communication, fun, and friendship—concentrate on creating conversation-friendly seating arrangements, and be sure to add comfort items. It's easier to invite friends over to join you in your tribal council when the setting is inviting and the atmosphere hospitable. Next, use the D.U.S.T. principle to clean the room and look for clues to the emotional dirt that may be lurking here (review the steps in chapter 10, House Rule #2: Keep it Clean).

Establish the new tradition of "Couch Council" (described at the end of this chapter) for ongoing work on developing relationships. It may be slow going at first, but as people warm to talking, their interest in it will grow, and your home may become the happening place of great fun and debate.

If this room is a HOTSPOT, target the applicable broken rule. Go down the whole list. Are there repairs that need to be addressed? Does the color make the room *pop*? Can you ratchet up the divine link with crown molding details? What about your COMING ATTRACTIONS and the goals you've identified for your life and your home? Can any of your future labels or desired titles be addressed here? Use the information you've been gathering to heal this room so it can bring your loved ones together.

RULES OF THE ROOM

1. Comfortable seating arranged to encourage conversation.

2. A focal point that pulls everyone toward the same center (*not* the TV).

3. Side tables or coffee tables within arm's reach from every seat.

4. Three kinds of lighting: warm overall/ambient, accent & task/reading.

5. Magazine racks to control paper clutter & caddy for remote controls.

6. No single individual has domain over the choice of entertainment or remotes.

Talking Heads—The Conversation Pit

Fellowship and entertainment are the practical functions of the living room, but increasingly this space has become a place where families and friends commune with video games and the television set instead of with each other. The result is an increasingly alienated society with a growing sense of disconnection. That is not to say that entertainment should not be shared. The recent explosion of home theaters brings a great opportunity for shared experiences filled with fun, laughter, and excitement. But your living room should be more than that. It should be the place where spirited discussions take place, book salons are held, and personal values are debated.

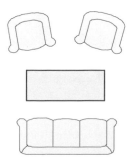

What does it mean to create a space that invites *camaraderie* but doesn't stifle speech or thought? It means that you don't sweep things under the rug, but rather, bring an open mind and warm heart to daily encounters here. You hold council and come to terms about family decisions … together. In this room, group dynamics depend on the layout of your furniture. Social scientists have identified *sociopetal* seating as an arrangement that encourages participation and communication—chairs that face each other and are not too far apart, but far enough to give some sense of personal space. In essence, you want to create a congenial conversation pit where comfortable chairs and sofas encircle a coffee table, with lamps for accent lighting that bring out everyone's best features and a focal point that puts everyone in an upbeat, talkative mood.

Isolation is achieved by separating the furniture by more than eight feet and facing chairs away from one another. These patterns discourage interaction—such as the kind of seating you might see in a waiting room. Is this what you've got? Are you going to create a shared identity here or fight over the remote from the bleachers of flanking Barcaloungers? Start a gentle revolution: create a space in the center of your house where others can connect with the *real* you.

The Elephant in the Room

Repairs always trump décor, but if something's broken in the living room, family room, or den, it's very likely your quality of life or your family unit. When people refer to the proverbial "elephant in the room" (that everyone ignores), they're often talking about the living room. Why? Because here the problem of even just *one* affects the *whole* household. Alcohol or drug abuse; debt, gambling, or sex addiction; mental illness, and so on, take up all the space in your common rooms.

Correspondingly, these issues respond best to *group* interventions—group therapy, support groups, or 12-step groups like AA—because they are afflictions that were frequently born in groups and take their toll on groups. It's the relationship with the group that needs help. Take a deep breath and summon the courage to call out that elephant and lead it out of the house, making living easier for everyone.

Even if the identified "problem" is not you, but a spouse, parent, or child, you and everyone else are still part of the problem, if for no other reason than you cannot escape it. That's called *codependence*, and your life depends on getting help. Get help for yourself even if the elephant is digging in. CODA (Co-Dependents Anonymous), Al Anon, Alateen, and ACOAA (Adult Children of Alcoholics Anonymous) are widely available self-help groups dedicated to recovering from the family dynamics that cause this kind of suffering. While there are therapeutic and religious alternatives, the above are good places to start—no matter where you are—because they ask for no commitment, no appointment, and virtually no money. Importantly, your privacy is certain. There's no need to suffer alone and in silence: Community heals family ills.

Living Room Requisites

REMOTE CADDIES: Table & armchair caddies help wrangle those remote controls.

FOCAL POINTS: Art & fireplaces, not high def plasma TVs, make excellent focal points.

BOOK JACKETS: The brush attachment on your vacuum is terrific for dusting tops of books.

CD ART: Corinthian CD storage pedestals hide your collection and provide a sculpture platform.

LIFE LIMITER: All-white color schemes limit activities. Use color to liven up the atmosphere.

CHIMNEY SWEEP: Fireplaces swept annually will avoid flue fires from creosote buildup.

MAGNETIC ATTRACTION: Electrostatic cloths wipe TVs and monitors clear of magnetic dust.

REMOTE WARS: Camaraderie & fellowship means no one gets to hog the remote!

EN GARDE! Scotchgarded furniture, spill-proof carpets & well-sealed floors are stress-proofers.

TO YOUR STATIONS: Create stations for video games, TV viewing, reading, or just hanging out.

STORAGE: Usable surfaces can also be storage areas—ottomans, coffee tables, side tables, etc.

TRIBAL ART: Art says, "This is who we are." Use art to share your "tribe's" interests & loves.

MISS MANNERS: Private behaviors belong in the bedroom or bathroom, not this public room.

WITHOUT SANCTUARY: The living room should never double as a bedroom. It impedes the function of the room and doesn't respect that individual's basic need for privacy and sanctuary.

A NEW TRADITION—COUCH COUNCIL

No one looks forward to a house meeting. It usually means someone is being read the riot act. Instead, call a weekly meeting everyone will look forward to. COUCH COUNCIL is a painless way to begin a tradition of family fellowship around the enjoyment of dessert and lively conversation. Once a week following a meal, retire to your tribal council where a different member will pick any topic they choose. Everyone will go around in turn and speak their mind on it for two minutes. No judgment is allowed of either the topic or any individual's opinions on it. Whether it's "Bullies at School" or "The Difference Between Self-Love and Vanity," everyone gets their time uninterrupted (even if it's two minutes of a five-year-old's "um ... um"). Go around your circle twice so you can add to your remarks after hearing what others have to say. It will develop your inner circle's sense of trust and attachment, deepen relationships, and develop young minds—while sharpening older ones.

We live in an age when forces are at work to dumb us down into agreeably submissive consumers—so create a space that invites camaraderie (but doesn't stifle speech or thought) and sweeten it with a little dessert. For half an hour each week, you get to think for yourself and share your insights with your friendly familiars while, at the same time, exercising listening skills. Keep your council strong and develop your own value system, not one dictated by TV pundits.

For a year's worth of stimulating TOPIC CARDS, check out our website.

Kitchen

THE HEARTH

PRACTICAL FUNCTION	EMOTIONAL FUNCTION
PHYSICAL SUSTENANCE	NURTURANCE

Your Hearth

The kitchen remains the heart of the home—the ancient hearth—where food is only part of what's served. Meal prep time is also the time when family news is shared and schedules, homework, and the state of each other's health, wellness, and grooming choices are discussed. The three most often heard words in the kitchen could just as easily be "You're wearing that?" as "What's for dinner?" And while the kitchen is not known for deep conversation, it often occurs here, late at night when everyone else is asleep or in the middle of the day when they're out, over a steaming cup. The kitchen is perfect for this kind of fulfilling conversation because it's where we are used to getting fed.

When quarreling, criticism, neglect, or abuse happens here (or has happened in this location in your past), it can affect your ability to nourish yourself and to care for others. When you live alone, remembering the meaning of this room—a warming fire—is crucial. There's a danger in the silence of a solo kitchen that will turn it into a chilly grazing ground where food is avoided, grabbed like rations, or devoured in a state of desperation, standing up. This is a cold hearth but need not be.

If your lifestyle is grab-and-run, there are plenty of quality prepared foods on the market to fill your larder, and no one has to cook an orange to eat one. Start nurturing yourself now by bringing sustenance in. Begin with a simple bowl of fruit on your kitchen table. Select only your favorites at the market. Then wash them immediately and place them on your table. A pretty bowl of fruit is food for art, ambience, and appetite—and a direct announcement to your cerebral cortex that you will be taken care of here. Then begin with just one meal: breakfast. There are now terrific appliances like the "3-in-1 Breakfast Maker" with a tiny toaster oven, griddle, and coffee maker that bring the whole task to one location. If your kitchen brings you only one sustaining meal a day, it has done its job. There's no emotional famine in an Emotional House.

You deserve support each day from an abundance of fresh options that nourish your body as well as your spirit. Observe these Room Rules in addition to the twelve House Rules.

RULES OF THE ROOM

1. A cozy nook for a light meal (even if it's a café table in an adjoining room).

2. A stool or chair for another person to perch on while food is prepared.

3. Three kinds of food available at all times (shop for these each week):
   - ✓ Something you can make quickly.
   - ✓ Something delicious and comforting.
   - ✓ Something nutritious.

4. Never allow yourself (or others) to eat standing up.

5. Keep it clean, keep it safe, keep it open to everybody.

The Flavor of Love

It's difficult to describe the flavor of love, but when a cookie is made with it, you certainly can taste it. Are there delicious flavors, smells, and sights that affirm love in your kitchen, or is your hearth a desolate wasteland of sterility, guilt, and resentment or a cesspool of filth, lack of support, and eating disorders? Kitchens are frequently EMOTIONAL ROLLER COASTER ROOMS. But you can turn around that dynamic. Bring art and beauty into your kitchen to make it a nurturing environment. And make it a fun personal rule to add something visually extraordinary to every meal. It doesn't have to be fancy; even a syrup smiley face on a pancake can elevate a dining experience. Dust desserts with powdered sugar or cocoa. Sprinkle finely chopped chives from your herb garden on the edges of a plate. Cut sandwiches on the diagonal. The Emotional House kitchen's aim is to transform food preparation, itself, into an emotionally nourishing experience, so you take pleasure in caring for yourself and your loved ones. Take the time to dress every single plate with a loving hand, whether you add a sprig of parsley or design a gourmet food tower. That love *will* go in.

A Functioning Kitchen Is All About Good Workflow

There are three primary meal-related tasks in a kitchen's workflow—preparation, cooking, and washing up. Good kitchens have balance at the core with a triangle formation that facilitates this workflow. Your own counter space, stove, and sink probably form a triangle of some kind, even if a slightly skewed one. You move naturally in the center of this triangle from sink to counters and fridge to stovetop. If your kitchen doesn't have this formation (if all three task areas are lined up in a row), you have a poor design that does not support easy meal preparation. If you feel stressed and aggravated when preparing meals, you'll taste it in the food it taints, too. A rolling prep surface, like a butcher block cart on wheels, can be moved into place in a pinch, giving you that golden triangle. And if your refrigerator door hits you the wrong way, switch its direction to harmonize with the flow of the room. It's easy to do. Check your manual.

Old Mother Hubbard's Kitchen Cupboard

Meals will be served in and from the kitchen, even if it's just takeout, so the room has to function for *physical sustenance* with proper plates, utensils, and washing accoutrements. Naturally, there must be food in your fridge and pantry shelves. Keep three kinds of food always on hand: something quick, something comforting, and something nourishing. This way, you send a message to your soul that your hearth has all your bases covered, and you will be nurtured, regardless of time pressures or emotional upheavals. Remember, fresh, unprocessed food is cheaper and tastes better than frozen and packaged foods. It takes only slightly more time to prepare, but you will be healthier and more nourished by it. (Check the Internet for recipes, starting with our website; and please, share one of yours.)

A cozy, warm kitchen, where the kids like to finish their homework while the parents are preparing dinner, helps support your Emotional House with a healthy heart. *Nurturance* means providing and receiving support and encouragement. You cannot overutilize the hearth, but you can abuse it, spoiling subjects that were once fresh by putting on too much heat and burning them to a crisp. You can certainly underutilize this room, too, starving yourself or your loved ones with neglect, deprivation, or control of all the choices. Eating disorders—overeating and anorexia—often relate to a lack of appropriate emotional support and the rage that eats at you in the face of a world that provides some with a banquet of love. Use your hearth as the site of reassuring words instead (make it a point to say some to yourself and your loved ones daily in this room) to combat these issues.

A Healthy Kitchen

Daily washing, wiping off, and scrubbing of the dishes, stovetop, sink, and counters is a health necessity—every day, every night. Rinse out your sponges and dishcloths in hot water with a little bleach frequently, and don't ever use them on the floor. You risk cross-contaminating your food supply with bacteria. The new disposable disinfecting wipes on the market come in handy before and after preparing poultry or meats that must be handled with extra care.

Clean your whole fridge and your oven thoroughly twice a year. Consult your manuals and follow the directions. For old freezers you have to defrost and newer ovens that clean themselves, you need to know the specific procedures and restrictions for keeping them in top condition. *Always* hire a licensed professional to do repair work on the gas lines of a gas stove. Refrigerators must also be in working order at all times. Spoiled food can mean a trip to the hospital or even a fatality if the diner is an infant, elder, or someone in compromised health. Many refrigerator parts can be replaced (condensers, thermostat assemblies, defrost timers, etc.), but a bad fridge risks putting toxicity in the same padded room as your food. Fix it or replace it immediately. As for broken or chipped dishes—call them art, because you can't use them for food anymore—they're homes for bacteria.

Of course, even your pots and pans can be hazardous if not maintained properly. If you're getting oddly grayish flakes of "cracked pepper," with a strange bland flavor, you may have served up Aunt Edith's Teflon mashed potatoes—not good. Not even the manufacturers of nonstick products recommend chips of it as spice. Don't ever use beaters in these kinds of vessels; use plastic spatulas to avoid scratching them; and never cook the water out and burn them, because there's *fumes* in those fumes (*perfluorooctanoic acid*, also known as C-8). If it's too late for that, and the nonstick surface is already damaged, discard it immediately. We prefer old-fashioned cast iron. It requires a little more maintenance than nonstick cookware, but it's worth it! Follow directions on pan seasoning, use coarse salt to clean it, and you've got yourself a nontoxic nonstick pan.

Like love itself, the kitchen can be a dangerous room where burns, cuts, and falls readily occur. Install stovetop guards to safeguard children from burns; put door locks on cabinets; keep sharp implements in a knife block and toxic substances in protected zones inaccessible to children. Do not let children play or sit anywhere within the triangle prep area. Install a runner on the floor to catch water splashes and prevent dropped glasses from shattering. Also use a safe, sturdy stepstool, instead of a tippy chair, to gain access to high cupboards. More falling accidents happen in the home than anywhere else.

A Homey Kitchen

This is not the room for empty promises. A "show kitchen" drains you of energy—it's a vacant thought that needs to be tended. Use your copper pans, hang your iron griddles, display your flours, pastas, and staples in airtight containers out in the open, get flour on your apron, *get real*, and enjoy the bounty of life.

Comfort food is the opposite of show—it can bring you back to balance when life is harsh. Know everyone's favorite comfort food in the house. When someone is down and can't cook or eat, appear before them with their cherished peanut butter and jelly sandwich or bowl of cheesy macaroni and spoon-feed them good cheer with balanced nutrition. If you're the cook of the house, teach others how to prepare their favorite comfort foods, so they can mature in their own self-care.

Put the favorite meal in a family heirloom (serving dish) and you've got a comfort food in a "Comfort Crutch." There is great emotional comfort in keeping traditions if you take the time to nourish them. But if your family of origin was toxic and critical, these are *not* Comfort

Crutches. So, start a new heirloom collection of gorgeous collectible serving ware and permeate it with positive values you hold dear.

Of course, comfort in the kitchen goes beyond edibles. Counters at a perfect height, padded kitchen chairs, and the weight, grip, and balance of the kitchen tools are increasingly becoming designed for comfort and ergonomic wellness. Some of these items might be advertised for crippled and arthritic hands, and thank goodness for tools that keep the kitchen accessible—however, they're more comfortable in all hands, so don't wait for gnarled knuckles before bringing them in. Additionally, a squat and sturdy stepstool for the height-challenged can save a backache when doing dishes and prep work. We'd like to see designers start incorporating pop-out stepstools right into cupboard design.

Dining Al Fresco

In the case of any major kitchen overhauls, create a "chuck wagon" kitchen outside during the construction. A gas barbecue with an attached burner can go a long way toward making an extended "cookout" a low-stress alternative to your normal routine. If you don't have a covered porch, rent a cabana and move your toaster oven, coffee maker, hot plate, and water cooler into the same area and get into the new culture. An ice chest or small fridge (you can also rent these) will keep your perishables alive. Kitchen makeovers are easier to take in the summers. They are notorious for running on for months, and dining al fresco can ease the discomfort.

What's Coming—The New Time Savers

Computer technology is about to take over the kitchen. "Smart appliances" are coming onto the market. Miele's award-winning Master Chef ovens now have computer programs that can memorize up to forty-eight of your favorite recipe settings and times. You key in the words "Mom's Apple Pie," and the oven does the rest, preheating to the right temperature, telling you when to put in the dish, and setting the timer. Just leave your kitchen-challenged family members a note to key in "Roast" and the oven will guide them through the rest while you're stuck in traffic. And TMIO's "Intelligent Oven" is a fridge and oven in one. It refrigerates your meal until it's time to cook it. You can even turn it on remotely with your phone or over the Internet.

Smart refrigerators will store computerized video recipes for you to follow with step-by-step instructions … and they'll create your shopping lists for you. Your appliance will soon record the bar codes on all the food that goes in and notify you on an LED screen on the front door when reserves are low. The time has come to get up to speed and start flexing your technological muscles.

A Delicious Kitchen

UNDER-CABINET STEMWARE & WINE RACKS: Utilize unused space under cabinets.

A MATTER OF FOCUS: A warm pendant lamp over a breakfast table creates an instant focal point.

FLOWERING FOOD: A painted window box herb garden brings beauty and flavor to your hearth.

PET PLACEMAT: Get dog & kitty placemats that fit your décor and feed your pets nearby, while you eat.

THIN WIRE RACKS: On the insides of your cupboards, create a food pantry even in a *small* kitchen.

CAFÉ & AGRICULTURAL THEMES: Complement the functions of giving & receiving care here.

RETRACTABLE COOKBOOK HOLDERS: Mount under cabinets & spring down when you need them.

TASTY FABRICS: Gingham, toile, striped and floral tablecloths & café curtains are delicious here.

TIERED LAZY SUSANS & SHELVING STEPS: Double your storage space inside cupboards.

THE ART ON YOUR PLATE: Add a diversity of colors, flavors (spices), and textures to every plate.

APPETIZING COLORS: Orange and yellow hues are believed to help aid digestion.

LARGE UTENSIL CROCKS: On countertops, keep spatulas, spoons, lifters & whisks at the ready.

TEACH EVERYONE TO COOK: It's a nurturing act to teach children & adults to care for themselves.

POT RACKS: Keep pans readily accessible *and* clear out a whole other cupboard for extra storage.

COLOR FLECKS: Pick colors in granite countertops to complement similar tones on walls.

SHOPPING LIST: Post a list on your memo board and allow everyone in the family to add to it.

CHILDREN'S ART: Traditionally associated with mothering, it belongs in the kitchen.

HOT POTATO: Keep meals hot by pre-warming plates with divine electric plug-in plate warmers.

CHINATOWN CHIC: Brighten your table with inexpensive serving ware from your Chinatown.

DISPLAY YOUR STAPLES: Decorative baker's racks dressed with ivy provide an attractive backdrop for staple containers.

A NEW TRADITION—COMFORT FOOD FEAST

Once a month, have a cooking party at which *everyone* makes someone else's favorite dish.

❈{ 25 }❈

Bathroom

THE TEMPLE BATH

PRACTICAL FUNCTION	EMOTIONAL FUNCTION
PURIFICATION	REVERENCE

Your Temple Bath

Like an ancient temple bath, this is where you reconnect with the purity of your spirit by removing the trespasses and temptations of the world from your body. This self-care is so fundamental, it should be approached with *reverence*.

We first experienced the various primal acts of bathing as infants when our mothers changed our diapers and bathed us in a basin. Whether your parents approached you with gentle sweetness, making these chores acts of love and care, or if they were judgmental, rough, or emotionally not present, is likely reflected in how you keep your bathroom temple and approach your own self-care today.

These energies still exist in the ways you experience the sacredness of your body, your sense of privacy during your solitary ablutions, and your deepest sense of safety when you're in vulnerable situations, as you are when in the bathroom. And this has everything to do with the way you now feel about the value of your being. You deserve to be greeted by a refreshingly clean bathing temple each time you go there. Whether you are taking your bathroom to the level of a pampering spa with heated floors, skylights, and a whirlpool tub; or using more simple steps, like adding color, plants, lighting, candles, scents, and music; the aim is to create an air of veneration that gives support to your efforts to put yourself together in whatever image your professional or social life requires, but from an authentic place within you.

RULES OF THE ROOM

1. A visual element of beauty that inspires you and boosts your morale.

2. Thirsty bath mats available to prevent slip-and-fall accidents after bathing.

3. Only 100% cotton towels—changed whenever soiled, and laundered weekly.

4. Sanitary pump-dispensed liquid soap available at all times.

5. Extra roll of toilet paper within reach of commode.

6. Trash receptacle and toilet brush discreetly on hand near commode.

7. Air freshener (spray/candles/plug-ins) handy, but safe from children.

8. Sink, tub, and toilet rinsed clean after *each* use.

9. A door with a lock that works.

Clean and Serene

"Pristine" is the only permissible standard for this most sacred of spaces in your home. Do your basin, bath, shower, toilet, floor, and accessories make you feel clean even as you enter

to cleanse yourself? Or do you hold your breath as you enter and get out as fast as you can, to escape the room's filth and, by extension, your own? It's surprising how many homes' bathrooms are fetid and putrid spaces, instead of rooms of purification and rejuvenation. You deserve to be greeted by a refreshingly clean bathing temple each time you go there.

Purification should be a rejuvenating experience, not a traumatic one. It feels personally violating to encounter waste others have left behind, so it is vital that all surfaces, mirrors, and porcelains remain sparkling and sanitary at all times. A toilet brush beside the commode encourages compliance. And the same goes for overspray of toilet bowls by little *and* big boys. There's nothing cute about festering bacteria and urine odor. Place disposable sanitizing wipes near the toilet and instruct offenders to use them each time they overshoot. It will encourage better aim and teach malefactors about respecting others.

Everyone should be required to *clean up* after themselves if they've left toothpaste globs in the drain, wet towels on the floor, or lingerie hanging from the shower door. Hair from shavers and hairbrushes should never linger in sinks. A common body mite, *Demodex folliculorum*, favors the human hair follicles of the face and ears—reason enough to keep those shavers and hairbrushes clean. Of course, clean means a fresh smell as well. A room freshener should always be handy. Scented votive candles make the room more agreeable for the next visitor. When everyone takes responsibility for keeping the purification temple hygienic and accessible, reverence becomes a standard of living.

Safety is Sacred

Next to the kitchen, the bathroom is the most dangerous place in your home. Accidents occur in this room frequently, so safety measures are vital. Bathroom plug outlets must be protected by a ground-fault circuit interrupter or GFCI—these are the ones with red and black buttons. Use only UL-rated blow-dryers, electric toothbrushes, and razors. Keep electronics well away from water sources. Remove medications from within reach of children and guests, and dispose of any that are past their expiration date (one year from dispensing). Install grab bars and nonslip mats in showers and tubs if elders or children are residents. And place childproof locks on toilet seats, hot-water faucets, and cabinets where toddlers have access. If physically challenged occupants use the bathroom, keep safety in mind and purchase shower chairs and lifts from a healthcare specialty store. Small children should never be left alone in a bathroom, even for a minute. Drowning and scalding are life-changing hazards. Set that boundary with them *and with their caretakers*.

Bathroom Essentials and Extras

SHOWER SQUEEGEES: Squeegee walls & glass daily to keep mildew at bay between cleanings.

PEARLY WHITES: Change toothbrushes every three months & sterilize often with mouthwash.

SILENCE IS GOLDEN: A fan or sound masker (music, fountain) relieves stress by offering privacy.

HELLO DUCKY: Playful bubble baths & rubber ducky pals are great bathroom Comfort Crutches.

FIGHT MOLD & MILDEW: Use only moisture-wicking hampers in your bathroom to avoid mildew.

NO FAKES ALLOWED: Show towels are no towels. Chuck appliquéd fakes; get absorbent cottons.

LITTLE GREEN APPLES: Great eating, but gross guest soap. Neutral aromas are much more welcome.

LIQUID SOAP: Buy refills in bulk to keep pump dispensers topped up at all times.

A FRIEND IN NEED: Extra toilet paper & discreet feminine items are a generous touch near the commode.

WE LIKE IT MOIST: Humidity-loving plants, like ivies, breathe life & warmth into cold bathrooms.

LIGHT UP YOUR DAY: A 7x magnifying mirror with super-bright lights aids makeup application.

AWASH IN COLOR: Repeat color and pattern in towels, curtains & bathmats to coordinate a look.

A WARM HUG: Electric towel warmers provide a warm hug from towels on cold winter mornings.

EVERYONE'S TEMPLE BATH: Assign hooks & shelves to everyone who uses the bathroom.

WETLANDS: Protect artwork from humidity. Mount art behind glass with a proper seal at back.

UNMENTIONABLES: Squeeze out water and hang lingerie on plastic hangers inside bedroom doors to dry.

NO PRESSURE: Pressure-assisted toilets quickly power flush your worries to the main line.

CHEMICAL FREE: April Shower Euro Filters provide 99% chlorine-free pH-balanced showers.

FLASH FLOODS: Turn off the water to the toilet and sink whenever you work on them.

EYE CANDY: Hand-painted, mosaic tile, and gilded basins elevate your cleansing rituals.

FAST FRAMES: Internet company MirrorMate sells peel-and-stick frames for bathroom mirrors.

NOW YOU SEE IT, NOW YOU DON'T: Séura TVmirror and Philips MiraVision use "smart technology" to incorporate video inside your bathroom mirror. When the TV's on, you'll see the screen image right inside the mirror; when it's off, you'll see a normal mirror.

A NEW TRADITION—THE *INNER* BEAUTY TREATMENT

If you struggle with your personal presentation or body image, or with spiritual malaise or emotional anxiety, or if you long for a sense of dignity about your life, chances are your bathroom is not presenting you with a strong foundation. Start to change that by using the room in a new way. Draw the eye to a reminder of the emotional function of the room—reverence for your life—by creating an arrangement of items that offers a positive message to your spirit—a bowl of polished stones or seashells that invoke the rejuvenating feeling of an ocean breeze and the elemental depths of life, for instance. Or mementos of your personal origins, such as photographs of your ancestors and so on. Bring in reminders of the purity and goodness of your body and themes that provide you with a sense of reverence for this precious body in which you travel through life.

This *inner* beauty treatment, a favorite of a longtime client, is a prescription for lifting your spirits. Take one once a month or as needed. Run a hot bath in a candlelit tub. Add an aromatherapy scent—scented candles, bath oil beads, drops of extract or essential oil, or fresh sprigs of rosemary. Slip in and relax. Breathe in the beauty of purity and light from its very source, knowing that you fill all your cells with these essences when you breathe. Allow the spirit of love to fill you, healing every offense and wounding word you've endured. Cast off all thoughts of shame or humiliation you may have experienced regarding your body or its most intimate and vulnerable functions. Let them sink to the bottom. Fill your mind with the realization that all life in its intricate distinctiveness is beautiful and completely acceptable. Feel the soft water's caress rolling over your skin, nourishing that fragile defensive armor. Understand that you were invited into this world and have a place in it. Fill every cell in your body with the beauty of that knowledge. When you're fully nourished, pull the plug and let all those undeserved feelings of unworthiness go down the drain.

⊰{ 26 }⊱

Bedroom

THE SANCTUARY

PRACTICAL FUNCTION	EMOTIONAL FUNCTION
SLEEP, SOLITUDE & SEX	INTIMACY

Your Sanctuary

Your bedroom is a sanctuary that restores your body and perspective with *sleep*, your mind and emotional equilibrium with *solitude* (whether reading in bed, meditating, writing in a jour-

nal, or just trying on clothes), and your spirit and life force with *sex*. Whether private or shared, this room has the job of meeting your emotional need for *intimacy*—with yourself as well as with another. Honoring intimacy as a real need will guide you in designing, decorating, and maintaining this room in support of that need. It also means you won't *live* in this room exclusively: you don't work in it, you don't eat in it, and you don't visit with acquaintances in it—unless you're sick and bedridden. The bed is the most intimate piece of furniture in your home. And that's where a lot of problems in and confusion around the bedroom congregate. Intimacy is not always appropriate—it needs to be protected. Thus the designation of *sanctuary*.

RULES OF THE ROOM

1. Adequate fresh air circulation.

2. Natural 100% cotton (or linen) bedding.

3. Two side tables (with compartment) for all beds larger than a single.

4. Bedside lamp and clock with lighted display.

5. A way to reach someone outside (cell phone, panic button, etc.).

6. Bench, wardrobe valet, or chair for extra blanket, robe, or tomorrow's clothes.

7. Security windows that can be restricted from opening wider than four inches.

8. No TV in the room.

Common Ground

If you are not in a productive relationship but would like to be, you need to set up your bedroom to support the functions of a sanctuary for *two*. Keep the room free of clutter and tasks that conflict with intimacy and get a bed that is large enough for two to stretch out comfortably.

For couples who share this room, conflicts of décor and space usage that are not worked out to each partner's satisfaction might reflect the power struggles and dissatisfactions that will eventually rot the bonds between you. Some women keep this room so frilly and ruffled, no man with any self-respect could call it a sanctuary. Conversely, men who decorate around the theme of a conquering lair strike a discordant chord with the women they are hoping to lure. You are not looking so much for a compromise in this room (where one concedes to the other) as for middle ground (the place where you can both agree). The balance lies somewhere between your individual selves, where your union resides.

What's important is that both partners feel represented, so that you can build your range for intimacy together. To accomplish this design task, use the exercises in chapter 7, Possessing Personal Style, to discover *each* of your own individual personal palettes. Be sure to include neutral colors. Then bring the two palettes together and see which favorites you share. If you can only come up with one color you both like, then that's your color—for wall, trim, and drapes. Yours will be a monochromatic color scheme, with variations appearing in shades and tones of the same color. Use the same exercise with furnishings, wood and fabric textures, and art.

In an interpersonal union, you can hold dear to the "I" while cultivating and nurturing the "we." The bedroom is the place in your home where the "we" comes together in the deepest, most profound manner. So find the common ground when designing and laying out the area and ensure that everyone has an equal amount of space for their belongings and their spirits, and an equal amount of responsibility for maintaining cleanliness, organization, and this room's sanctuary status. Women should not take the lion's share of the closet, even if they tend to be clothes horses. This room is about sharing, and that means even-steven. Sorry, gals, you can't *own* the room where your mate sleeps, too.

Protecting Your Sanctuary

Your time in this room is essential to your physical, mental, and spiritual health; it lends support to your emotional equilibrium, your experience of wellness, and your will to live—you must not let anyone cut you off from it because of your lack of willingness to close the door and set limits. Let kids know what the closed door means. A door that locks and sound masker that confines the sounds generated inside, to the inside, are vital in this most private of rooms. Unless you're the parent of an infant or a toddler who must be supervised at all times, this room should be sacrosanct from children when that door is closed.

Fearfulness, exhaustion, illness, allergies, and insomnia are afflictions associated with this room that can be comforted, battled, or assuaged by handling problems with the room itself. If you have been sexually violated here or elsewhere, as one in four women and one in seven men reportedly have been, this is probably an EMOTIONAL ROLLER COASTER ROOM for you. It is paramount that you take this room back as a sanctuary. The book *Spiritual House-cleaning* (2001) offers an in-depth healing journey for violations in general, and this room in particular. The Emotional House Program directs you to keep going and embrace intimacy once again. Check into your feelings by using the D.U.S.T. method of cleaning your room mindfully. Write down (or draw) the story of any violations and disappointments around the topic of intimacy. Place the written story of your violation or bad experience in an envelope. Label it "Bad Memories I Won't Allow to Affect My Future Happiness" and address it to the Bureau of Understanding. It's difficult to separate yourself from the negative experiences of your life and this is a symbolic exercise, true. But if you acknowledge and add your story to the virtual database of human atrocities and injuries, others may one day figure out a way to stop committing them.

These events are not the things that need to define your whole life. Store the envelope in your keep (basement, attic, or garage), or anywhere outside of your sanctuary. Then spend time working on this room. Turn your bedroom into a healing, restorative sanctuary as a way to defy any violations you experienced around the issue of intimacy. Loving yourself is the first step toward that healing. Protect intimacy by putting limits on who is allowed in this room and the kinds of interactions accepted here.

While kids' and dorm rooms tend to have desks in them, the bedroom is not a good place to put your home office—unless you want to kill the softer parts of you that unite with your larger soul or another human being. However, if you need to multifunction this room, the second function—especially if it is a computer or work station—needs to be set off by screens or tall plants or something else that turns the space into two separate rooms. This is a boundary you need to set with yourself.

Pajama Games

You have to be careful about dragging the quality of intimacy into every other activity besides the appropriate ones. You have spent at least a third of your life since birth sleeping in your bedroom, and your body—including your voice—is in pajamas ... or less. If you think you're concealing that from people on the other end of the phone with whom you're conducting business, you're wrong. They might not picture you in your birthday suit, but they sense that something's "not right," especially when formal business discourse degrades into inappropriate familiarity. It is inappropriate to hold business meetings in the boudoir, especially in person. Those tasks are out of harmony with the function of sanctuary, forcing visitors, who feel their own sense of intimacy violated, to squelch feelings of embarrassment.

Tuning Out

Okay, TVs. We realize many people use them in the bedroom for many reasons—sleeping aid, company, and foreplay, primarily. And if you're going to break a rule, this will probably be it. But, consider that the use and function of this room are at odds with the use and function of the TV.

Nothing against television—one of us watches more than enough, while the other is responsible for putting quite a bit of it on the screen. We just think you should be fully conscious of what the medium is all about and, more importantly, fully conscious when you're watching it. Remember that everything you see and feel when watching it—advertising, news, drama, comedy, reality—is *manipulating* you through your senses to elicit a certain thought, reaction, or feeling. Its number one function is as a marketing tool; entertainment comes second. Programs are "packaged" for impact and the medium tells you when to laugh, cry, and feel hungry, and what to do about it, as well as what to purchase immediately. And most of us cooperate in predictable patterns. That's what makes it such a powerful tool. It's important that viewers remain conscious and alert when watching it, and that's not the mood you should be in while settling down in your bedroom. So tune out.

One-Third of Your Life

Recuperative *inactivity* requires one-third of every day to be effective, so owning a quality mattress should be a major priority. You need physical support from the bed, cleanliness, lighting, and comforts here. If you wake up with backaches, experience eyestrain while trying to read, or choke with stale air, make changes to transform this room into a fresh and restorative space.

Because the body sloughs off dead skin and hair when you sleep or change dirty clothes, dust is a major problem in the bedroom. That means dust mites—a primary cause of allergic attacks—are in abundance. Launder the sheets, sweep, vacuum, or mop the floor (including under the bed), and dust everywhere *every* week. Use dye and perfume-free detergents and softeners for laundering your linens and try to use as few chemical cleaners in this room as possible. We do not recommend upholstered headboards or headboard draperies—they are havens for dust mites. Use protective allergen barrier encasings—like the Breathe Right brand—for mattresses and pillows. It's also a good idea to clean the *air* in this room with a HEPA air cleaner. Nothing works better to help remove airborne dust and mites, supporting your breathing all night long.

Sanctuary Substantials

A SNUG FIT: Measure mattress width, length & *depth* before buying sheets. Sizes vary.

CALIFORNIA KINGS: (Cal-Kings) are longer than Eastern Kings and excellent for tall individuals.

EASTERN KINGS: Are wider than Cal-Kings and slightly roomier for cramped couples.

EGG-CRATE FOAM MATTRESS PADS: Are cheaper to replace than a worn-out mattress pillowtop.

HIGH THREAD COUNT 100% EGYPTIAN COTTON SHEETS: Breathe, don't pill & soften with age.

NO CHEMICALS: Place natural linens on the bed, hot from the dryer, and you won't have to iron.

SLIDING WINDOW LOCKS: Security locks limit window openings while allowing fresh air in.

SOUND CONDITIONER: Marpac's white noise emulator, SleepMate, offers restful sounds of water.

IRRITABLE INFANTS: Marpac's LifeSounds soothes newborns with familiar womb sounds.

MARRIAGE SAVER: Sleep-Eze's Snore Buster uses hearing aid technology to mask noise.

ON THE NIGHT SHIFT: Thrifty blackout liners fit underneath draperies and block excess light.

ELECTRONIC-DRIVE ROLLER SHADES: Lutron's Sivoia QED blocks light at the flick of the switch.

SPACE CHALLENGED? Utilize under-bed storage space with self-enclosing dust-free containers.

BEDSIDE SADDLEBAGS: Eyeglasses, books, lotions, and other private items not-for-display fit here.

SLEEK WARDROBE VALETS: They make the next day's clothes inviting and stress-free.

FORBIDDEN FAMILY: Don't want your parents in bed with you? Don't display their photos here.

INTIMATE DISCRETION: Contain intimate items in decorative boxes or drawers of bedside tables.

SENSUAL AMBIENCE: A spray of candles is an invitation to romance.

DECORATIVE FINIALS: These turn bland curtain rods into divine details.

CEILING ART: This is the one room where you lie back and stare at the ceiling. Make the view scenic.

HOT CLIMATE? Pick cool colors for the bedroom to cool the room (violets, greens, and blues).

COOL CLIMATE? Choose cozy warm colors to heat up passions (orange, yellow, and red hues).

A NEW TRADITION—RELATIONSHIP REPAIR DATES

Everyone has a bad patch now and then and could use some help. Try a Relationship Repair Date (or Personal Repair Date if single) when you feel things falling apart. Spend two hours in your sanctuary together (or alone, if single) focusing solely on fixing what feels wrong, not pointing out what's broken. Light some candles, put on soft music, and put yourself into a state of curiosity as you deepen your connection to your partner or to yourself. The theme for these repair dates is *dreams*.

Talk, cuddle, and reveal to your partner (or journal by yourself) your most recent or your most powerful dream—the dream you had for your life before today, before you met, the dream you have for your shared life now, the kind of sex you dream of having; and your innermost desires and deepest thoughts about life. Spending authentic time with yourself and your partner is how you build intimacy and mend the broken connections of your life or marriage, a repair ritual well worth repeating.

Home Office

CENTRAL RECORDS

PRACTICAL FUNCTION	EMOTIONAL FUNCTION
BUSINESS OF THE FAMILY	VALUE & ACCOUNTABILITY

Your Central Records

Your home office is the hub for your Emotional House's finances, where the *business of the family* is handled, and it is central to your *accountability* for the space you take up on this planet.

People used to be able to keep and pay their bills easily at the kitchen table, but that was when there were only a few utility payments and a mortgage or rent payment to keep track of. Today, our economy is increasingly service driven and the paperwork has risen exponentially. Multiple service contracts (mobile phones, cable, Internet, security alarm response, pest control, furnace maintenance, housecleaning), subscriptions, memberships, bank fees—it all adds up. Multiply these by the IRS, requiring detailed records, and the stress quotient around finances is clear. Your household is a mini corporation. You need a home office, not just to fulfill the business of the family but to meet the emotional function, which is the dignity and *value* you receive when you demonstrate accountability for your consumption. Face the reality of being a grown-up and get the equipment listed below in the Rules of the Room. Then chuck that shoebox mentality of keeping tax receipts and the idea that money is not a big deal.

RULES OF THE ROOM

1. All files and office equipment easily within reach.

2. An ergonomic task chair that tilts and adjusts in height.

3. A desk with comfortable leg room and sufficient workspace.

4. Adjustable task lamp to avoid glare and eyestrain.

5. A place to display your TO DO list, FIVE-YEAR PLAN, and budget.

6. Filing folders and unit (or banker's-style file box) to contain receipts.

7. An easy-to-use accounting system (either computerized or paper ledger).

8. Shelving, storage containers, and ascending files for organization.

9. Sunlight, greenery, and beauty elements to remind you why you work.

Setting Up Your House Accounts

Every home needs an organized filing routine and an accounting system, or your accountability starts to slide and the creditors descend, bringing harassing phone calls, letters, and misery as they remove your self-esteem, good credit, and financial privileges one by one. This conflict will dislodge the cornerstones of your Emotional House and internal conflicts will erupt. Money is the number one issue couples argue about and break up over. Becoming a mature, contributing member of your family—and society—means learning to strategize and chart your future with action steps that lead to a logical conclusion. In this way, you take responsibility for your choices and attain dignity in your trustworthiness and answerability for your excesses.

Organize and maintain your accounts to get an accurate picture of your spending habits versus your tangible income; then you can make the proper shifts to keep your balance (emotionally and financially) and stay within your true means. If you don't have a filing cabinet, get a $5 cardboard banker's-style file box with a lid and some hanging folders from your local office supply store. Take a Saturday to make permanent account categories for your new filing cabinet for each home expense frequently incurred. Common categories are listed on the next page.

Common Household Expense Categories

AUTO (GAS, REPAIRS, INSURANCE)	INSURANCE
BOOKS & SUBSCRIPTIONS	INVESTMENTS
CABLE	MEALS & ENTERTAINMENT
CHARITABLE DONATIONS	MEDICAL
CLOTHING	MORTGAGE/RENT
COMPUTER ACCESS	OFFICE SUPPLIES
DUES & LEGAL FEES	POSTAGE
EQUIPMENT & SUPPLIES	PROPERTY TAXES
GIFTS	REPAIRS & MAINTENANCE
GROCERIES	TELEPHONE
GROOMING	UTILITIES

Put them in alphabetical order in your new "filing cabinet." You'll only have to do this *once*. As you pay your bills throughout the year, write the date and amount you are paying and the check number on each receipt and deposit it into its respective category's file folder. If you pay by phone or Internet, write down the confirmation number.

When your canceled checks are returned from the bank, get in the habit of dropping them into the appropriate category file folder too, always placing the most recent addition at the back of your pile so they will remain in date order. This will take only minutes each month. But now you have proof of all your payments and, come tax time, your records are already presorted for you by date and category.

At the end of the year, remove the receipts from their folder, clip them together by category, and keep them with your tax documents in an envelope. This way you start the new year with empty file folders in your cabinet, ready for the next year's receipts. You'll really love this system when you need to find an old receipt for a warranty issue. There's no digging through an unruly shoebox, you just find the tax year, leaf through to the category, and boom, you've got your hands on it. That's stress-free financial maintenance!

You must keep accurate financial records for tax reasons, and better records mean more bona fide tax deductions—why should corporations get all the tax breaks?

But what about balancing those accounts? Read the back of your bank statement; it explains the steps. We highly recommended a wonderful software program called Quicken, which will not only ease the pain of balancing, but also give you an instant snapshot of your spending habits to see where your budget problems originate.

Destination Success!—Tackling and Completing Your Projects

In addition to accounting, your home office should serve any entrepreneurial efforts or personal projects you tackle. Stay-at-home moms are joining this force at such an alarming rate they've got a name: *mompreneur.* But if you have difficulty completing your projects, or run out of creative juice along the way, you are not alone. There are many individuals with talent, work ethic, and motivation in spades whose ventures break down anyway and never get finished. Here's a success strategy for completing your endeavors if creative blocks come your way.

Make a Progress Chart to pinpoint your breakdown point. You do this by mapping out your project like a road trip. Your journey has a beginning, a middle, and a destination. This doesn't have to be fancy. A simple road map of the stops along your project's path will work—idea stage, production, selling, and so on. Make charts for previous projects you never finished as well. Compare them. Where do you break down? After the idea stage, midpoint in creation, the production phase, selling, promotion, or somewhere else? By keeping progress charts, you identify where your efforts tend to run out of gas. This point on your journey is like a desolate part of the road with no filling station. You need to address the issue of running out of gas *before* you get to the place where you normally break down. (Go through the same routine if financial issues are a problem for you: Where do you break down? At the budget stage? Remembering to keep receipts? Entering receipts? Balancing the checkbook? Writing the check? Find your failure point. Then you can find a solution.)

Whether your work chugs to a halt because of a fear of rejection, a need for perfection (which is really the same thing), a lack of information or skill, or because you just simply *hate* doing that part of the work, the following remedies offer tools to get your motor running again:

1. REFOCUS YOUR GOAL: Change your goal from "producing a *perfect* end product" to mere *"output."* As we say in the literary field, "Don't get it right, get it written."

2. ATTAIN KNOWLEDGE: Get a book or take a seminar to acquire the know-how to get over this hump with new skills. The stimulation will rekindle your passion.

3. SEEK ASSISTANCE: Subcontract a piece of the project out, hire an assistant, or form a partnership with someone who can pick up the ball where you've dropped it

(maybe that math whiz kid of yours can balance that checkbook for you). What may be pure drudgery to you may be pure joy to another.

Though you pay a price for all of these remedies, the cost of not fulfilling your goal and achieving success is higher. Use Progress Charts and get help instead.

Extra Office Tips

SCHEDULED BACKUPS: Computers crash and data disappears. Use a software backup program.

L-SHAPED OR COCKPIT-STYLE DESKS: These shapes are best for high-workload home offices.

CHEAP SHELVING: Dress it up with pretty baskets and boxes. Be sure to label them.

TASK LAMPS: Cast light over the work area, not into your eyes or onto your computer monitor.

FLAT SCREEN COMPUTER MONITORS: They take up less desk space, leaving you more work area.

HIGH-SPEED BROADBAND INTERNET: It'll soon deliver movies to your home. Get hooked up now!

WARMER COLORS: Reds, oranges & yellows are optimistic colors that stimulate the mind.

ACHIEVEMENT ART: Goal boards, awards, plaques, diplomas, and degrees inspire work efforts.

CLOSET CONVERSION: Hide an office space inside a closet with a sliding door. Organize vertically.

TICKLE FILES: File bills a week before due date in your monthly calendar to tickle your memory.

SHRED NOW, DON'T PAY LATER: Shred all financial documents you are disposing of to avoid identity theft.

CHILD'S PLAY: Create a child's office inside yours. They can emulate you & remain in view.

Q-TIP CLEAN: Dip them in rubbing alcohol to clean up sticky keyboards or your computer mouse.

DESK POSTURE: Your back, elbows, and knees should be at a 90° angle, with arms relaxed.

A NEW TRADITION—REPAIR YOUR RELATIONSHIP TO WORK AND MONEY

If this is an EMOTIONAL ROLLER COASTER ROOM for you, things have gotten out of whack in your relationship to money, work, and priorities. Refer to your FIVE-YEAR LIFE PLAN to remind yourself of the big picture. It is your responsibility to service all areas of your life. If you're out of work, in crushing debt, and at a loss as to how to fix the situation; or if you work all the time and have no downtime; or if you can't manage your affairs because you've never had to do a darned thing for yourself ... make a list of everything you're good at and all the things that you like to do. If sewing, comforting and patching up a child's boo-boos, selling anything, giving speeches, baking, sleeping on the couch, driving, writing, making widgets, or something else is what you love to do or are good at, write it down. Divide the list into three categories:

- Things you believe could give you financial compensation

- Things that give you the emotional reward of contributing to others

- Your guilty pleasures

For those who do too much, working and giving away all your time, you need to indulge in some *guilty pleasures* and release some of your duties. For those brave enough to admit to a sense of entitlement, you need to dip into the *contribution* column and experience the gifts of service. No riches are greater. And if you need a boost in income, review your starting list of things you love to do that are in the *potential compensation* column. There are entrepreneurial opportunities there. Yes, there are! Martha Stewart built a multi-million-dollar business doing what she loved and started out by selling pies she baked in her own kitchen.

Begin brainstorming with a pen and paper and use your home office as a research center to begin assembling data about markets and products and how to build a business plan. Perhaps yours will be the next patent, the next hot new subscription service, or the next multi-million-dollar public offering on NASDAQ. Just remember, doing something you love is the best way to earn income, because the work becomes your pleasure, not your punishment.

❦ 28 ❧

Additional Rooms

THE *REAL* ESTATE

The Rest of Your Rooms

Unfortunately, we don't have space to explore every possible room in these pages, but you now have the tools to identify their meanings to you, the practical and emotional functions they fulfill, and how they measure up to the Four Cornerstones of an Emotional House. Use the twelve House Rules in every room to elevate their feel and function. When you approach these and other additional rooms, use the notes you've kept in your *Emotional House Design Binder* and keep one thing in mind: your home has all the answers to your questions. Just open your eyes and check in with your heart.

Dining Room

THE ROUND TABLE

PRACTICAL FUNCTION	EMOTIONAL FUNCTION
COMMUNION	BONDING

Your Round Table

While eating occurs in the dining room as it does the kitchen, the Round Table is linked to formal dining in a special setting. Even the customary family dinner here is on a different level from any meal in the breakfast nook. It is a time of official and deliberate *communion*—of coming together and *bonding* over common ground. Breaking bread here is more ceremonial, and connections here are both more soulful and more measured than anything else you do in your house.

The only word in our culture for the heightened atmosphere possible here is *brotherhood*, hence the reach back to the Knights of the Round Table for this room's meaning. But it's not about brothers, it's for everyone, including sisters, children, and elders. If yours isn't, you have the kind of dining room in which too many families fall apart. Conflict at the Round Table—with hostility and scorn swallowed along with meals—will destroy your Camelot just as it did King Arthur's. Eating and fighting don't mix. Further, marriages and families often break apart due to a lack of bonding that makes outside temptations inviting. When the glue holding families together is strong, temptations to abandon or betray have little appeal. Create that atmosphere here.

RULES OF THE ROOM

1. The table is the focal point—keep it clear and wiped clean, ready to be set.

2. Keep centerpieces low, never impeding eye contact.

3. Cloth napkins and dripless candles set the proper tone: well-mannered.

4. Comfortable, straight-backed chairs with boosters for smaller diners.

5. No arguing allowed—take conflicts to the living room and debate there.

A NEW TRADITION—EVERYONE COUNTS

Each mealtime, allow every person at the table to relate something that happened in their day.

Kids' Rooms

THE FORT

PRACTICAL FUNCTION	EMOTIONAL FUNCTION
NURSERY/HIDEOUT	BECOMING

Their Fort

It's not your room, it's theirs. Free, thinking citizens develop in free spaces that they become responsible for. That's why this room starts as a *nursery* where the tiny shoots are tended and evolves into a *hideout*, where the older rebels can plot their uprising. It has to be done; even you did it. This is the space where they are *becoming* who they will one day be—in spite of, in reaction to, or with the guidance of their home environment. As Kahlil Gibran wrote in *The Prophet*, "They come through you, but they are not from you, and though they are with you, they belong not to you." So keep them safe and let them be.

Childproof toddlers' and infants' rooms—cap plug outlets, add corner cushions to hard edges, and strap bookshelves and dressers to walls. Always read labels to see what chemicals your baby is sleeping on or in. Some baby mattresses still have phosphorus, arsenic, and antimony in them, reported to release toxic fumes when brought to body temperature or soaked with urine, possibly causing risks to health and life. The Emotional House Program watchwords remain: pure and natural is always best. Install colorful interlocking rubber floor mats in play areas where rambunctious play occurs. And create reachable organizing systems for clothing and toys that teach youngsters respect for their personal space. Let them pick out their daily ensembles the night before and place them on their child-sized wardrobe valet, a routine that will also help them establish good personal care practices.

Don't fight with teens about mess; give them a robot—the Roomba Floor Vac is a cordless self-propelling vacuum, shaped like a small flying saucer, that spins around the floor vacuuming *by itself*, guided away from stairs, furniture, and walls by infrared sensors. Higher-end models—costing around $200—have intelligent features, including an automatic return to the battery dock for a recharge whenever the battery is low.

RULES OF THE ROOM

1. Childproof everything! Visit the Good Housekeeping page on iVillage.com for a comprehensive checklist of tips.

2. Include furnishings that double as tools for playing and learning.

3. Choose a colorful palette and artwork that stimulates, soothes, and inspires. Go on a color discovery field trip with your child to stimulate their personal style muscles.

4. Student desk (follow Home Office Rules) for children who are homework age.

5. Hypoallergenic rug, floor pillows, and blankets.

6. Organizing cubbies that don't pinch little fingers and match height and age. Plastic cleans well and stands up to children's rough and tumble spirits.

7. Laundry hamper (include delivering it to laundry room in your Chore Chart).

8. Small-sized flashlight for fort play and safety during the night.

9. Privacy—as appropriate to their age.

10. Let kids decorate it and maintain it the way they want it (enforce city health code compliance, but otherwise just close the door, if it's awful).

11. No TV in the fort; it encourages isolation (see Bedroom Rules). And until homework requires separate units, keep kids playing together on a communal computer for pleasure use.

A NEW TRADITION—STORY TIME EVERY NIGHT ... GUARANTEED

Create bonding routines, like story times before bed in the fort for youngsters. When you work late or the babysitter is there, they can still have their nightly story with you if you just take a half hour to record it on audiotape in advance. Fisher-Price's Tuff Stuff Tape Recorder is under $20 and kid friendly, with big colorful buttons little fingers can push to hear Mommy or Daddy's voice whenever they need to.

Studio/Workshop

LABOR & DELIVERY ROOM

PRACTICAL FUNCTION	EMOTIONAL FUNCTION
CREATIVE ARTS	EXPRESSION

Your Labor & Delivery Room

Creating artwork—whether with paint, glass, fabrics, clay, stone, ceramics, weavings, metal, wood, photography, dance, theatre, or music—should get a room of its own. If this work is in the dining room, chances are you have to clean up before project completion. Creating the space for art gives permission to develop your soul's *expression*, without which it is mute.

No one person is simply one thing: not "just" sales personnel or housewives or mechanics or businesspeople. We are mothers *and* painters, fathers *and* musicians, students *and* entrepreneurs, filing clerks *and* photographers, waitresses *and* dancers, performance artists, sculptors, writers, and more. Pigeonholing yourself or anyone in your family doesn't allow for the vastness of human potential. The true census of who you are is to be discovered; a studio space is the place where you can begin to draw a more complete picture of your being. It's a birthing process; honor it with a room.

RULES OF THE ROOM

1. If no natural light is available, add a skylight or natural-spectrum lighting.

2. Good air circulation.

3. The tools of the trade for your arts of choice and lots of worktable space.

4. Soundproofing.

5. A ShopVac.

Display your work in your home. Hold an in-home exhibition, with beverages and friends. Celebrate your creative spark, and whenever you complete a project, dance a little jig.

Laundry Room

THE RIVER

PRACTICAL FUNCTION	EMOTIONAL FUNCTION
WASHING & FOLDING CLOTHES	NEW BEGINNINGS

Your River

How could a laundry room have a meaning? It's a laundry room, for Pete's sake! You know its practical function—*washing the clothes*, obviously, and if you're lucky enough to have a big enough room, folding and ironing them, too. But if you dismiss the emotional function, you may be pounding your clothes on the rocks in a dingy and dirty basement, or mistaking your bathroom shower rod for a tree branch on the banks. Is that why the whole family has you doing their laundry? This room is where the future flows out of the past. It absolutely gives you *a new start*. And guess what? Washing is not women's work. It's now the duty of everyone who gets things dirty! Even little kids are capable of folding.

Your laundry room may be decentralized, with areas of laundry handled in different parts of the house. Nonetheless, you need a clean room, light, art, divine details to weather the chore, and organizing solutions—a place for laundry products and stackable baskets for dirties and cleans awaiting folding. Vacuum out dryer vent lines frequently to prevent lint fires, and add a shutoff valve at eye level to your washer's rubber hose line to prevent flooding if intake lines deteriorate where you don't see them. You've got a river coming through; you don't want your house to be the floodplain.

RULES OF THE ROOM

1. Clean it when you clean the rest of the house.

2. Stackable baskets to accommodate workflow—dirty, clean, folded, colors, whites, etc.

3. A table (it can fold up or retract onto the wall) for separating and folding.

4. Plenty of sunlight and greenery (use natural-spectrum lightbulbs if this is in a windowless room).

5. Music—a CD player or radio will bring the life back into this room that your hatred of folding tries to kill.

6. Indoor retractable clothesline or drying rack for hanging/laying out hand wash. (A divine detail that keeps hand wash out of sight: Maytag's new Neptune Drying Center. It has an upper drying cabinet above the conventional dryer, with drying shelves and hanging rods, that prevents shrinkage by using air circulation and a minimal amount of heat.)

A NEW TRADITION—A SONG RUNS THROUGH IT

When people washed clothes by the river, the tradition was to sing glorious songs to ease the mundane chore. From this day forward, fill your laundering duties with music—whether from a radio, CD, or your own wonderful voice.

Basement/Garage/Attic & Storage Closet

THE KEEP

PRACTICAL FUNCTION	EMOTIONAL FUNCTION
STORAGE	REMEMBRANCE

Your Keep

Depending on what kind of storage you've got—from heavy family baggage to real tools you can use—these *storage* centers can feel like a dungeon, a museum, or a treasure trove. Make your choice and upgrade your Keep into a place to honor your history and, as the poet Robin Morgan suggested, "Disown none of your transformations." Do this by what both organizers and psychologists call *compartmentalizing*: Put things in their proper perspective and in their proper place, labeling them for recognition, *remembrance*, and retrieval; protecting them from theft and destruction; and protecting yourself from sharp edges and personal significance.

RULES OF THE ROOM

1. Use pest-resistant storage solutions (well-built shelves, sturdy containers).

2. Label storage containers with permanent markers and arrange by function.

3. Fireproof (no combustible materials near electric switches or pilot lights; fire extinguisher available and accessible at doorways).

4. Keep tools handy; financial records safe for seven years (as the IRS requires); feel-good mementos accessible; and your sad, bad, or regretful memories (that you can't quite throw away) boxed, labeled, and safely compartmentalized out of your way.

A NEW TRADITION—7 YEAR ITCH

Purge your Keep every seven years. Shred financial records that are out-of-date. Replace broken tools you've been planning to fix and review your Yuck Box. You might be surprised to discover you no longer need to keep it.

The Garden

EDEN

PRACTICAL FUNCTION	EMOTIONAL FUNCTION
CULTIVATION & HARVESTING	SERENITY

Your Eden

Peace and tranquility are the gifts given to you by this outdoor room. This is not about having a green thumb. We need to spend at least some time outside every day in the sun, in the rain, and in the dirt to be healthy and to feel good about our lives. The space of a garden—whether it's an expanse of lush green or prairie, cultivated or wild, a tiny piece of ground, or a container of soil under a Gro-Lite—brings you to the basis of what it is to live: to come from seed, to struggle, to sprout, to break through, to send out shoots and good gracious glory, to bloom! And, then, as if blossoming isn't everything and plenty enough in

its exuberance and joy, to bear fruit, to *produce* something—food that tastes like sun and rain and divinity, but that if left to its own devices will simply grow into more life. And that is the basis of what it is to live in an Emotional House, the space that is growing you.

But why does connection to this process of *cultivation and harvest* bring *serenity*? Because there is in it the understanding that that's all you need: a little dirt (and who doesn't have plenty of that), a few rays of light (and even the worst day offers some), and a sprinkling of rain, and if left to your own devices, you will grow into something. Eventually you will bloom and finally produce something delicious or brilliant and fulfilling. What a relief. Anything is possible.

Practice Parenting

Planting something that feeds you is an exercise in risk-free parenting. The fruits and vegetables we are sold in supermarkets have become flavorless imitations of their former selves, picked before ripe, and devoid of the sweetness and basic nutrition given to us through creation. Take back your garden and reexperience the cornucopia of delights that are free to all who dare to partake, and you will never agree to live in anything but an Emotional House again. Even a tiny apartment balcony or window can be filled with potted vegetables and flowering plants. Seed and nectar feeders will encourage songbirds and hummingbirds to visit and stay awhile.

Plant seeds of potential growth—nurture and care for something over an extended term, witness growth and tend the weeds, and ultimately reap the rewards of fruits born—without the tendency for them to end up in therapy. Cultivating such living things brings a tangible reward that in turn feeds and teaches us gratitude. And creating an Emotional House is about creating space not only for ourselves, but for the gifts of the larger community, including the earth.

When working in your garden, put yourself in the mind of planting the seeds of your future in the same way. Make plans for taking action over the long haul to nurture your dreams' seeds into the fruit that will feed your spirit. Begin with your garden, then apply these lessons to your life, and you will be well fed.

RULES OF THE GARDEN

1. Put your garden in your eyes every day and spend half an hour outdoors (wear sunscreen).

2. Plant and harvest something that feeds you, even if it's chives in a window box or a potted tomato plant on a balcony.

3. Bring fresh flowers into your home *every* week, all year round, even if it's a single carnation from the grocery store.

Your Outdoor Room

Your outdoor room might need to serve several masters—sports, family activities, exercise, garden, and dining area, to name the most common. Separate your play areas or patio gym from your serenity areas with potted ficus, queen palms, or benches and the like. Interlocking rubber mats (GymCor sells them through home improvement stores) can create a springy outdoor floor that will keep your equipment safe and offers another terrific demarcation solution. As for ball playing—away from windows still holds.

If you entertain a lot, the larger barbecues have side panels to hold dishes while you cook. Propane grills are great because of their instant-on, instant-off capabilities (use only out-of-doors), and the absence of starter fluid in the grill flavors. You'll still need a water spray bottle to knock down fat drip flare-ups and a fire extinguisher for more serious fire hazards. The higher-end grill islands now have side burners built right in, and in some cases, refrigerators, deep fryers, serving buffets, wine coolers, food warmers, built-in ice drawers and ice-makers, and *more*. Provide your own chef.

The Green Thumb Group

From the desertlike low-water maintenance of *xeriscaping* to the lush, water-thirsty English cutting garden redolent with vibrant blooms and flitting butterflies, to a compact apartment-sized window box of basil, parsley, and chives, your choices are manifold. Make sure the scope of your Eden falls within your time commitment. Your garden should be a joy, not a drain. Remember, a perfect manicure isn't necessarily a perfect garden, especially when the fragrance is pesticide. Gardens should be filled with the songs of wild birds and the buzzing of bees servicing flowers, or it's not a garden, it's a chemical waste site. Go green with your pest control products whenever you can—organic is better eating for wildlife and wild minds alike. Sprays sold under the brand name Safer contain insecticidal soaps that don't harm plants or animals, but do discourage the tiny pests that eat your shrubs and blossoms.

The hard-core garden enthusiast might consider a backyard greenhouse. From $300 for a great little starter size upwards to thousands, these offer double-thickness polycarbonate glazing with automatic vents that open to prevent overheating. When you consider the ongoing costs of plantings every new season, the value of growing your flowerbeds, tropical plants, and organic salads from seed makes it well worth the one-time cost. Wireless thermometers are available to monitor greenhouse temperatures from inside the house.

For those with fatter wallets, an insulated sunroom, solarium, or English conservatory (with a pitched roof and bayed front) will allow indoor/outdoor use year-round and allow you to begin seedlings well before planting season. Often less costly than an ordinary addition, with today's new insulated windows, these are now practical in any climate. Check out the higher-roofed orangeries—they allow you to plant a fruit tree indoors!

Garden Delights

FIRST THINGS FIRST: Buy a dining-height table set first. You'll get the most use out of this.

CURB APPEAL: Realtors reveal that a mature tree means $10,000 of value added to your home.

BENEFICIAL BUGS: Ladybugs and lacewings feed on destructive garden pests, naturally.

TAKE IT WITH YOU: Sew foam patches into the knees of your garden trousers for a kneepad on the go.

DULL AS DIRT: Sharpen lawn mowers at the start of the season & garden tools throughout.

CHAISE LONGUES: The comfort is all in the cushion depth and adjustability of the back.

HANDSOME HARDSCAPES: Attractive edging helps frame your garden canvas.

STRIKING SOFTSCAPES: A curved garden bed edge makes any garden look more natural.

PLAY BALL: Pond barley balls (floating ball with barley straw) cleans surface algae from ponds.

OUTDOOR AIR CONDITIONING: MistyMates' superfine mist cools the air outside as much as 30°.

BONE DRY: The DryGuy boot & glove dryer air-heats boots dry at a low 99° from the inside out.

BICYCLE HOOKS: Hanging bikes keeps patio & garage floor areas free and tires from going flat.

DEADLY TO DOGS: Snail bait, rat poison & weed killers cause 43% of domestic animal poisonings.

THIRTEENTH-CENTURY SPHERES: Historic iridescent gazing globes reflect beautiful garden views.

ZEN DEN: A meditation bench tucked into a corner of the garden makes it a room of one's own.

POETIC SENTIMENTS: DIY stone kits with press-in letters turn pathways into thoughtful passages.

EXPLOSIVE NEIGHBORS: Store pool chemicals (chlorine and muriatic acid) apart from each other.

UP IN SMOKE: Wire-brush first & then preheat on high to burn off residual BBQ grime.

LEAVE IT OUTSIDE: Boot scrapers and garden clogs keep the dirt where it belongs.

EXTERIOR ART: Plaques, friezes, metal sculptures & even decorative mailboxes can beautify.

ALMOST AUTHENTIC: New shatterproof polycarbonate plates and glassware mimic real crystal.

NO-MAINTENANCE FURNITURE: Aluminum-frame sling chairs last 6 to 7 years before deterioration.

WARM AS TOAST: Outdoor propane heaters extend your outdoor season for months.

SLIVER SHIVER: Sand and varnish wooden tool handles at the beginning of each season.

CUSHION COORDINATES: Use house brick or trim color for cushions to harmonize your look.

POOL PH: Get a new pool testing kit every year. Testing solutions lose accuracy with age.

GROUNDED: Sticky yellow White Fly Glue Traps that hang on trees are death traps to all birds.

WHAT'S OLD IS NEW AGAIN: Rusty patio furniture can be powder-coated to restore its beauty.

TWELFTH NIGHT: Tiny white holiday lights on an arbor turn shadows into an enchanting garden.

MAN OVERBOARD: Pool surface safety alarms sound when glassy water surfaces are disturbed.

TABLETOP ZINC PATIO BURNERS: Citronella gel repels mosquitoes and provides a fire element.

SWALLOW SHOWER: Bland birdbaths become water features with solar-powered fountain spouts.

FLOWER PLAY: Violets & blues married with yellow are dramatic color choices for borders.

ETCH A SKETCH: Before planting, sketch out a color scheme and plan for the whole garden.

ALOHA: Thatch on patio umbrellas and a few bamboo torches turn a backyard into a Hawaiian village.

PRIVATE BEAUTY: Shrubbery, trellises & water features block unwelcome eyes with beauty.

COMPLEMENTARY COLOR SCHEMES: Flowers in concentrated patches create a spectacular effect.

SHADY DAYS: Market umbrellas mean you can entertain longer outside on hot and wet days.

A NEW TRADITION—THE MAGIC HOUR

The magic hour is the time of day when the sun is at its lowest in the sky and the light is at its loveliest—an hour either just before sunset or just after sunrise. Filmmakers call this the *magic hour* because the sky offers a rich soft glow, and the heavens become a magical bluish/purple color—wonderful for filming and flattering for skin tones. Everything and everyone looks so much better in this light.

If you're feeling down, depressed, anxious, emotionally frazzled, or angry, the fastest way back to center is to spend some time in greenery with the voice of nature whispering in the leaves. The business of life can disconnect us from the serenity we experienced in childhood, when, with our backs to the earth, we stared up at the heavens and contemplated cloud formations sliding across the sky. We need these experiences in our adult lives to reconnect with the basic gifts of creation. So, with a hot or cold beverage in hand, head outdoors either as your day begins or as it ends, and inject a few minutes of serenity into each day. You will find that all things will begin to look a little brighter too. There is something healing about looking at the big picture of life. And from here, the perspective of your Emotional House looks even brighter.

Resources

GREAT WEBSITE LINKS

NO PINK TOOLS ALLOWED:
TomboyTools carries lightweight (not pink), solid, woman-sized tools, and offers great home improvement techniques too.
www.tomboytools.com

FABRICS BY MAIL:
Hancock's of Paducah sells tons of terrific fabric and remaindered bolts at discount Internet prices. A very responsive delivery system and excellent fabric index.
www.hancocks-paducah.com

HOME OFFICE & FITNESS CENTER IN ONE:
Hidden Grove Furniture combines the armoire desk and exercise treadmill in a space-saving solution.
www.iconfitness.com/icon/HiddenGrove

PEEL & STICK BATHROOM MIRROR FRAMES:
MirrorMate sells peel and stick frames that turn any flat mirror "into a beautiful, framed focal point." They cut to order and deliver by mail. They even have videos to show you how to measure and install it.
www.mirrormate.com

MAKE YOUR OWN POT RACK:

Ubuild offers instructions on making a great pot rack with just ceiling hooks, stainless steel chain, a few S hooks, dowels, and wood pieces.

www.ubuild.com

DIY:

If you're a do-it-yourselfer, this website is worth a visit for your next construction or decorating project.

http://doityourself.com

FREE VIDEO TRAINING:

Lowe's provides interactive online DIY tutorials with spoken instruction and moving pictures to show you step-by-step techniques on everything from hanging drywall to patching dead grass to installing a curtain valance.

www.lowes.com

CHILDPROOFING:

Good Housekeeping tips for childproofing your home & kids' rooms are here:

http://magazines.ivillage.com/goodhousekeeping/myhome/housecare/spc/0,,284551_295397,00.html

EXERCISE MATS:

GymCor, "the web's largest selection of gym equipment," sells fitness equipment and interlocking rubber mat flooring (mega-lock) that is great for your patio gym, child's playroom, garage or recreation room.

http://gymcor.com/exfloormat.html

A TV INSIDE YOUR MIRROR:

Séura's television mirror means you don't have to miss the morning show while putting on makeup or shaving.

www.seuratvmirror.com

TAKE IT WITH YOU FIREPLACES:

Apartment dwellers can own a real flame fireplace that burns odorless alcohol gel.

www.apartmentdecorandmore.com/pofimo.html

References

Beeton, Isabella Mary. 1861. *The Book of Household Management.* (Available now from Southover Press, 1998.)

Gibran, Kahlil. 1923. *The Prophet.* New York: Knopf.

Maslow, Abraham. 1943. A theory of human motivation. *Psychological Review,* 50: 370–396.

McGraw, Phillip C., Ph.D. 2000. *The Life Strategies Workbook.* New York: Hyperion.

Morgan, Robin. 1976. "The Network of the Imaginary Mother." *Lady of the Beasts.* New York: Random House.

Robyn, Kathryn L. 2001. *Spiritual Housecleaning: Healing the Space Within by Beautifying the Space Around You.* Oakland, Calif.: New Harbinger Publications.

Sullivan, Bev. 2004. As quoted by Jenny Deam. Tidiness trend riffs on desire for simpler life, May 31, 2004. Denver, Colo.: *The Denver Post.*

Kathryn L. Robyn is author of *Spiritual Housecleaning*, a consultant on healthy home living, master in Reiki healing, and editor for a national healthcare magazine. She has led transformational workshops and facilitated support groups in healing issues for over twenty years, working with organizations such as Child Help USA, the Alcoholism Center for Women, and Alive and Well, Inc., as well as in private practice. Her support groups for artists and adult survivors of child abuse and her popular workshops help individuals transform defeating habits, reframe personal obstacles, and repair trauma and spirit-related injuries. She offers workshops and personal consultations for those wishing to create a more supportive, nurturing, and inspiring home.

Dawn Ritchie is a consultant and a television writer and producer with credits on over fifteen network and syndicated dramatic series. Codeveloper of the Emotional House Program, she brings her visionary design, personal style development, and life-skills techniques to the book.